I0003439

Learn Data Analytics For Beginners

Data Analyst, Deep Learning, Neural Network, Python Data Analytics

BY

Landon Adrian

ABOUT THE BOOK

Data science has taken the world by storm. Every field of study and area of business has been affected as people increasingly realize the value of the incredible quantities of data being generated. But to extract value from those data, one needs to be trained in the proper data science skills. The R programming language has become the de facto programming language for data science. Its flexibility, power, sophistication, and expressiveness have made it an invaluable tool for data scientists around the world. This book is about the fundamentals of R programming. You will get started with the basics of the language, learn how to manipulate datasets, how to write functions, and how to debug and optimize code. With the fundamentals provided in this book, you will have a solid foundation on which to build your data science toolbox. In this book you will learn what you need to know to begin assembling and leading a data science enterprise, even if you have never worked in data science before. You'll get a crash course in data science so that you'll be conversant in the field and understand your role as a leader. You'll also learn how to recruit, assemble, evaluate, and develop a team with complementary skill sets and roles. You'll learn the structure of the data science pipeline, the goals of each stage, and how to keep your team on target throughout. Finally, you'll learn some down-to-earth practical skills that will help you overcome the common challenges that frequently derail data science projects Reproducibility is the idea that data analyses should be published or made available with their data and software code so that others may verify the findings and build upon them. The need for reproducible report writing is increasing dramatically as data analyses become more complex, involving larger datasets and more sophisticated computations. Reproducibility allows for people to focus on the actual content of a data analysis, rather than on superficial details reported in a written summary. In addition, reproducibility makes an analysis more useful to others because the data and code that actually conducted the analysis are available.

TABLE OF CONTENTS

Hello everyone and welcome to this interesting session on data science full course. So before we begin let's have a quick look at the agenda of this session.

AGENDA LIST

Evoluation of Data
Introduction to Data Science
Data Science Careers and Salary
Statistics for Data Science
What is Machine Learning
What is Deep Learning?

So first of all, I'll be starting off by explaining you guys about the evolution of data how it led to the growth of data science, machine learning, AI. all the different aspects of data. Then we'll have a quick introduction to data science, understand what exactly it is then we'll move forward to the data science careers. the salary and understand what are the different job profiles in the data science career path how to become a data scientist data analyst or a machine learning engineer. Then we'll move on to the first and the foremost part of data science which is statistics and after completing statistics. we'll move on to machine learning where we'll understand what exactly is machine learning what are the different types of machine learning and how are they used and where have they used the different algorithms. and next we'll understand what is deep learning and how deep learning is different from machine learning, what is the relationship between AI, machine learning and deep learning in terms of data science. understand how an exactly neural network works, how to create a neural network and much more, So let's begin our session now.

Data is increasingly shaping the systems that we interact with every day, whether you are searching Something on Google using Siri or browsing your Facebook

EVLUTION OF DATA

Feed you are consuming the result of data analysis. It is increasing at a very alarming rate where we are generating 2.5 quintillion bytes of it every day. Now that's a lot of data and considering there are more than 3 billion Internet users in the world a quantity that has tripled in the last 12 years and 4.3 billion cell phone users that are a heck lot of data. and this rapid growth has generated an opportunity for new professionals who can make sense out of this data. Now given its transformation ability it's no wonder that. So many data arrays with jobs have been created in the past few years like data analysts, data scientists, machine learning engineers, artificial intelligence engineers and much more.

And before we dwell into the details of all of these different professionals, let's understand exactly what data science is.

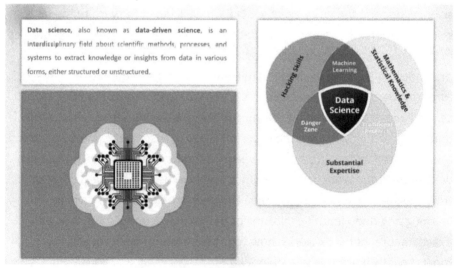

So data science also known as the relevant science is an

WHAT IS DATA SCIENCE?

Interdisciplinary field about scientific methods, processes, and systems to extract knowledge or insights from data in various forms. It's structured or unstructured. It is the study of where information comes from what it represents and how it can be turned into a valuable resource in the creation of business and IT strategies.

WHAT IS DATA SCIENCE?

Data science, also known as **data-driven science**, is an interdisciplinary field about scientific methods, processes, and systems to extract knowledge or insights from data in various forms, either structured or unstructured.

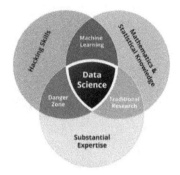

So data science employs many techniques and theories from fees like mathematics, statistics, information science as well as computer science.

and can be applied to small data sets also yet most people think data science is when you are dealing with big data or large amounts of data. So this brings the question of which job profile is suitable for you.

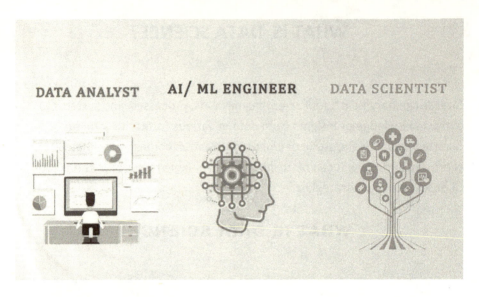

DATA ANALYST   AI/ ML ENGINEER   DATA SCIENTIST

is it the data analysts, the data scientist or the machine learning engineer. Now

CAREER : DATA SCIENCE

Data scientist has been called the sexiest java 21st century. nonetheless, data science is a hot and growing field so before we drill into the data science let's discuss all of these profiles one by one. see what this role are and how they work in the industries So read a science career usually starts with mathematics and stats as the base which brings up the force proflle in our data science career path which is a data analyst. So Idina analyst delivers value to the companies by taking information about specific topics. then interpreting analyzing and presenting the finding in comprehensive reports now

DATA ANALYST

Many different types of businesses use data analysts to help as experts data analysts are often called on to use the skills. tools provide competitive analysis and identify trends within the industry's most entry-level professional interested in going into Data related jobs start off as data analyst qualifying for this role is as simple as it gets all you need is a bachelor's degree in computer science mathematics. a good statistical knowledge strong technical skills would be a plus and can give you an edge over most other applicants. So next we have data scientists there are several definitions available on data scientists but in simple words, the

DATA SCIENTIST

Scientist is one who practices the art of data science the highly popular term data scientist was coined by DJ Patton. Jeff hammer backer data scientists are those who crack complex data problems with strong expertise in certain scientific disciplines they work with several elements related to mathematics statistics computer science and much more now data scientists are usually business analysts or data analysts with a difference it is a position for specialists. you can specialize in different types of skills like speech analytics text analytics which is the natural language processing image processing video processing medicine simulation material simulation now each of these specialists roles is very limited in number. hence the value of such a specialist is immense now if we talk about AI or machine learning ingenious. So machine learning engineers are sophisticated programmers who develop machines and systems that can learn. apply knowledge without

MACHINE LEARNING ENGINEER

Specific direction artificial intelligence is the goal of a machine learning engineer they are computer programmers but their focus goes beyond specifically programming machines to perform specific tasks now they create programs that will enable machines to take actions without being specifically directed to perform those tasks.

SALARY TRENDS

So now if we have a look at the salary trends of all of these professionals so starting with a data analyst the average

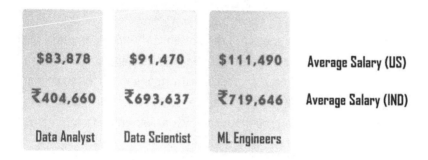

$83,878	$91,470	$111,490	Average Salary (US)
₹404,660	₹693,637	₹719,646	Average Salary (IND)
Data Analyst	Data Scientist	ML Engineers	

salary in u.s. is around 83,000 dollars or it's almost close to eighty-four thousand dollars whereas in India it's around four lakh. four thousand rupees per annum. Now coming to data scientist the average salary is ninety-one thousand dollars nine eleven points five thous. dollars and in India it is almost seven lakh rupees and finally four ml in ten years the average salary in u.s. is around one hundred. eleven thousand dollars whereas in India is around seven lakh and twenty thousand dollars. So as you can see the radius scientist an ml ingenious position are a certain higher position which requires a certain degree of expertise in that field. So that's the reason why there is a difference in the salary of all the three professionals.

MARKET TREND: MACHINE LEARNING

So if you have a look at the road map of becoming any one of this profession. So what the first one needs to do is own a bachelor's degree now this bachelor's degree can be in either computer science mathematics information technology statistics finance or even economics now after completing a bachelor's degree the next comes is fine-tuning the technical skills during the technical skills is one of the most important parts in the roadmap where you learn all the statistical methods and packages you either learn are Python essays languages which are very important you learn about data warehousing business intelligence data cleaning visualization reporting techniques walking knowledge of Hadoop. MapReduce is very very important and if you talk about machine learning techniques it is one of the most important parts of the data science career now apart from these technical skills there are also some business skills which are very much required. So this involves analytical problem-solving effective communication creative thinking as well as industry knowledge now after fine-tuning your technical skills. developing all the business skills you have the options of either going for a job or either going for a master's degree or certification

programs now I might suggest as you go for a master's degree as just coming out of the BTech world. having technical skills is not enough. So you need to have a certain level of expertise in the field. So it's better to go for any masters or Ph.D. programs which are in computer science statistics or machine learning you can also go for big data certifications. you can also go for industry certifications regarding the data analysis machine learning or the data science it so happens that arica also provides a machine learning data analysis as well as a data science certification training they have master's program which is equivalent to a master's degree which you get from a certain University. So do check it out guys I'll leave the link to all of these in the description box below and after you have completed the master's degree what comes is working on the projects which are related to this field. So it's better if you work on machine learning deep learning or data ethics projects that will give you an edge over other competitors while applying for a job scenario. So a certain level of expertise in the field is also required and this is how you will succeed in the rate of science career path there are certain skills which are required which I was talking about earlier the technical skills. the nontechnical skills now if you talk about the skills which are required to become all of these professions.

DATA ANALYST SKILLS

So they are mostly the same so for any data analyst, first of all, you need to have analytical skills which involve Maths having good knowledge of matrix multiplications the Fourier transformations. all next we have communication skills. So come looking for a data analyst require someone who has the good communication skills who can explain all of their technical terms to non-technical teams such as marketing or the sales team another important skill required is critical thinking you need to think in certain directions. gain insights from the data. So that's one of the most important parts of a data analysts job obviously you need to pay attention to the details. So as a minor shift or the deviation in the result or in the calculation what you say the analysis might result in some sort of loss of the company it's not necessary to create a loss but it's better to avoid any kind of deviation from the results. So paying attention to the detail is very very important. then again we talk about the mathematical skills knowing about all the types of differentiation and integrations is going to help a lot because you know a lot of machine learning algorithms as I would say are mostly mathematical terms or mathematical functions. So having good knowledge of mathematics is also required apart from this the usage of technical tools such as Python are we have essays you need to know about the big data ecosystem how it works the HDFS how to extract data create a pipeline you know about JavaScript a little. if you talk about the skills of data scientist it's almost the same having analytical and statistics knowledge now another important part here is to know the machine learning algorithms as

DATA SCIENTIST SKILLS

It plays an important role in the data science career from solving skills obviously now another important aspect if you talk. about the skill which differs from that of a data, the analyst is only deep learning so deep learning I'll talk about deep learning later in the second half or the latter part of the book. So having a good knowledge of deep learning and the various frameworks such as sensor flow PI torch you have piano all of this is very required for data scientists. again business communication as I mentioned earlier is very much required because as you know these are one of the technical roles most technical roles in the industries and the output of these roles or what I would say the output of what these professions - is not that much technology is more business oriented. So they have to explain all of these findings to either the non-technical teams the sales the marketing.

ML ENGINEER SKILLS

Again you need the technical tools and the skills now for machine learning engineer obviously programming languages having good knowledge of our Python C++ or Java it's very much required you need to know about calculus. statistics, as I mentioned earlier learning about mattresses integration now another important skill here, is signal processing. So a lot of times machine learning engineers have to work on robots and signal processing they work on human-like robots they work on robotics which mimic human behavior. So a lot of signal processing techniques are also required in this field applied mathematics as I mentioned earlier. again neural networks it is one of the bases of artificial intelligence which is being used and again we have natural language processing. So as you know we have personal assistants like Siri and

17

Cortana. they work on language processing and not just language processing you have audio processing as well as video processing.

DATA SCINCE PERIPHERALS

So that they can interact with a real environment and provide a certain answer to a particular question. So these were the skills I would say for all of these three roles next if we have a look at the peripherals of data science. So, first of all, we have statistics needless to say there are programming languages we have short read integrations then we have machine learning which is a big part of data science and then again we have big data. So let's start with statistics which is the first area of data science or I should say the first milestone which we should cover.

WHAT IS DATA?

So for statistics let's understand first what exactly is data. So data in general terms refers to facts and statistics collected together for reference or analysis when working with statistic it's important to recognize the different types of data. So data can be broadly classified into numerical categorical and ordinal now data with no inherent order or ranking such as gender or race is called nominal data. So as you can see in type 1 we have a male-female that Is nominal data now data with an ordered series is called ordinal data. So as you can see here we have an ordered series where we have the customer IDs and the rating scale no data with only two options series is called binary data now in this type of data there are only two options like either yes or no or true or false or 1 or 0. So as you can see here we have customer ID and in the owner or car column we have either yes or no now the types of data we just discussed under law describe the quality of Something in size appearance value or something such kind of data is broadly classified into qualitative data now data which can be categorized into a classification data which is based upon counts there is only a finite number of values possible. the values cannot be subdivided meaningfully is called discrete data. So as you can see here in our example we have an organization and the number of products. So this cannot be subdivided into number of sub-products right and if you talk about data which can be measured on a continuum or a scale no data which can have almost any numeric value and can be subdivided into finer and finer increments is called continuous data so as you can see here in patient ID we have weight of the patient it is 6.5 kgs now kgs can be subdivided into grams and milligrams and final refinement is also possible now this type of data that can be measured by the quantity of something rather than its quality is called quantitative data now that we have honest with the different types of data qualitative.

VARIABLES & RESEARCH

Quantitative it's time to understand the types of variables we have now there are majorly two types of variables dependent and independent variables. So if you want to know whether caffeine affects your appetite the presence or the absence of the amount of caffeine would be the independent variable and how hungry you are would be the dependent variables. So in statistics dependent variable is the outcome of an experiment as you change the independent variable you watched what happens to the dependent variable whereas if you talk about independent variable a variable that is not affected by anything that you or the researcher does usually plotted on the x-axis now the next step after knowing about the datatypes and the variables is to know about population and sampling and that comes into experimental research now in experimental research the aim is to manipulate an independent variable and then examine the effect that this change has on a dependent variable now since it is possible to manipulate the independent variable experimental research has the advantage of enabling a researcher to identify a cause and effect between the variables well suppose there are 100 volunteers at the hospital and a doctor needs to check the working of a particular medicine which has been cleared by the government. So the doctor divides those hundred patients into two groups of

50 and then asked one group to take one type of medicine and the other group to not take any medicine at all and then after of me then compare the results and in non experimental research the researcher does not manipulate the independent variable this is not to say that it is impossible to do. So but it will either be impractical or it will be unethical to do. So, for example, a researcher may be interested in the effect of illegal recreational drug views which is the independent variable on certain types of behavior which is the dependent variable however why is possible it would be unethical to ask an individual to take illegal drugs in order to study what effects this hat on certain behaviors it is always good to go for experimental research rather than non experimental research.

POPULATION & SAMPLING

So next in our the session we have population and sampling those are two of the most important terms in statistics. So let's understand these terms. So in statistic, the term population is the entire pool from which a sample is drawn statistician also speak of a population of objects or events or procedures or observation including such things as the quantity of the number of vehicle owned by a penny person now population is thus an aggregate of creatures things cases. soon and a population commonly contains too many individuals to study conveniently an investigation is often restricted to one or most samples drawn from it now a world chosen sample will contain most of the information about a particular population parameter but the relationship between the sample and the population must be such as to allow true inferences to be made about a population from that sample for that we have different types of sampling techniques. So in probabilities, there are sampling methods which are classified either as probability or nonprobability. So in probability sampling each member of the population has a known nonzero probability of being selected probably the methods include random sampling systematic sampling and stratified sampling whereas in nonprobability sampling members are selected from a population in some non-random manner but these include convenience sampling judgment sampling quota sampling and snowball sampling while sampling is important there is another term which is known as sampling error. So sampling error is a degree to which a sample might differ from the population when inferring to population results are reported plus or minus the sampling error now in probability sampling there are three terms which are random sampling systematic sampling and stratified sampling. talking about random sampling probability of each member of the population to be chosen has an equal chance of being selected such type of sampling is random sampling never talk about systematic sampling it is often used instead of random sampling and it is also called the NEP name selection technique now pay attention to the name called Anette name. So after the required sample size has been calculated every NS record is selected from the list of the population member now its only advantages over Anna's having technique is its simplicity now the final type of sampling is stratified sampling. So a stratum is a subset of the population that shares at least one common characteristics the researcher first hand you fire irrelevant status and their actual representations in the population before analysis. So now that we know how our data is and what kind of sampling is done let's have a look at the measure of a center which helps describe to what extent this pattern holds for a specific numerical value.

MEASURES OF CENTER

So as you can see in measure of center we have three terms which are the mean median and mode and I'm sure everyone must be aware of all of these terms

MEASURES OF SPREAD

I'll not get into the details of these terms what's more important is to know about the measure of spreads now a measure of spread sometime called a measure of dispersion is used to describe the variability in the sample or population it is usually used in conjunction with a measure of Center tendencies

MEASURES OF SPREAD

such as the mean or median provide an overall description of a set of data now if you talk about deviation it is the difference between each X I and the mean for a sample population which is known as the deviation about the mean whereas variance is based on deviation and entails computing squares of deviation. So as you can see here we have the formula for the variance which is the difference between the mean and the particular data point squared and divided by the total number of data points and it's summation standard deviation is basically the under the root of variance.

MEASURES OF SPREAD

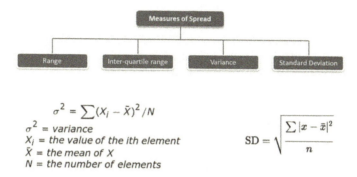

$$\sigma^2 = \sum (X_i - \bar{X})^2 / N$$

σ^2 = variance
X_i = the value of the ith element
$\bar{X}$ = the mean of X
N = the number of elements

$$SD = \sqrt{\frac{\sum |x - \bar{x}|^2}{n}}$$

So as you can see the formula is the same just we have the under root over the variance.

SKEWNESS

So that stood evasion and variance another topic in probability and statistics is Kunis. So skewness is a measure of symmetry or more precisely the lack of symmetry. as you can see here we have left skewed symmetric nonsymmetric left skewed we have right-skewed. normally distributed curves are the most symmetric curves we'll talk about normal distribution later.

CONFUSION MATRIX

So after skewness what we need to know about is the confusion matrix now confusion matrix represent a tabular representation of actual versus the predicted values now this help us find the accuracy of the model when we are creating any machine learning or the team learning model to find the accuracy what we do is plot a confusion matrix.

CONFUSION MATRIX

		Predicted	
		Good	Bad
Actual	Good	True Positive(D)	False Negative(C)
	Bad	False Positive(B)	True Negative(A)

You can calculate the **accuracy** of your model with:

$$\frac{\text{True Positives} + \text{True Negatives}}{\text{True Positives} + \text{True Negatives} + \text{False Positives} + \text{False Negatives}}$$

So what you need to do is you can calculate the accuracy of your model with adding the true positives and the true negative and dividing it with the true positives plus true negatives plus false positive plus false negatives that will give you the accuracy of the model. So as you can see in the image we have good bad for predicted as well as actual and as you can see here the true positive D and the true negative a are the two areas where we have created it it was good and the actual value was good in true negative we have the predicted it was bad and the actually it's bad. So model which gets the higher true positive and true negatives are the ones which have higher accuracy.

PROBABILITY

So that's what confusion matrix is, for now, the next term and a very important term in statistics is a probability. So the probability is the measure of how likely something will occur it is the ratio of desired outcomes to the total outcomes now if I roll a dice there are six total possibilities one two three four five and six now each possibility has one outcome. search has a probability of one out of six now for instance the probability of getting a number two is one out of six since there is only a single two on the dice now when talking about the probability distribution techniques or the terminologies there are three possible terms which are the probability density function normal distribution and the central limit theorem. the probability density function is the equation describing a continuous probability distribution. it is usually referred to as PDF now if we talk about normal distribution.

the normal distribution is a probability distribution that associates the normal random variable X with a cumulative probability the normal distribution is defined by the following equation. So as you can see here Y is 1 by Sigma into the square root of 2 pi 2 whole multiplied by E raised to power minus X minus mu whole square divided by 2 Sigma square where X is a random normal variable mu is the mean and Sigma is the standard deviation now the central limit theorem states that the sampling distribution of the mean of any independent random variable will be normal or nearly normal if the sample size is large enough now accuracy or the resemblance to normal distribution depends on however two factors the first one is a number of sample points taken and second is the shape of the underlying population now enough about statistics if you want to know more about statistics and I will talk about the p-value is the hypotheses what all are required or any data science project. let's move on to our next part of data science learning which is learning paths which is machine learning. so let's understand what exactly is machine learning.

WHAT IS MACHINE LEARNING?

Machine learning is an application of artificial intelligence that provides systems.

WHAT IS MACHINE LEARNING?

Machine Learning is a class of algorithms which is data-driven, i.e. unlike "normal" algorithms it is the data that "tells" what the "good answer" is

Getting computers to program themselves and also teaching them to make decisions using data
"Where writing software is the bottleneck, let the data do the work instead."

the ability to automatically learn and improve from experience without being explicitly programmed now getting computers to program themselves and also teaching them to make decisions using data where writing Software is a bottleneck let the data do the work instead now machine learning is a class of algorithms which is data driven that is unlike normal algorithms it is the data that does what the good answer is.

26

FEATURES OF MACHINE LEARNING

If we have a look at the various features of machine learning. first of all, it uses the data to detect patterns in a data set and adjust the program actions accordingly it focuses on the development of computer programs that can teach themselves to grow and change when exposed to new data.

FEATURES OF MACHINE LEARNING

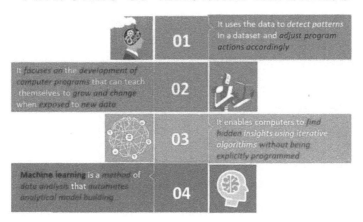

It's not just the old data on which it has been trained. So whenever a new data is entered the program changes accordingly it enables computers to find hidden insights using iterative algorithms without being explicitly programmed either.

HOW ITS WORKS?

So machine learning is a method of data analysis that automates analytical model building now let's understand how exactly it Wells. So if we have a look at the diagram which is given here we have traditional programming on one side we have machine learning on the other.

HOW IT WORKS

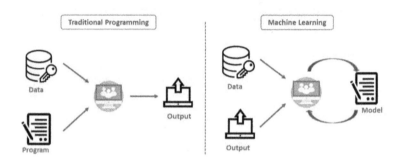

First of all in the traditional program what we used to do was provide the data to provide the program and the computer used to generate the output. things have changed now So in machine learning what we do is provide the data and we provide a predicted output to the machine now what the machine does is learns from the data find hidden insights and creates a model now it takes the output data also again and it reiterates and trains and grows accordingly. that the model gets better every time it's a strain with the new data or the new output.

APPLICATIONS OF MACHINE LEARNING

So the first and the foremost application of machine learning in the industry I would like to get your attention towards is the navigation or the Google Maps.

APPLICATIONS OF MACHINE LEARNING

So Google Maps is probably the app we use whenever we go out and require assistant in directions and traffic right the other day I was traveling to another city and took the expressway and the math suggested despite the havoc traffic you are on the fastest route no but how does it know that well it's a combination of people currently using the services the historical data of that fruit collected over time and a few tricks acquired from the other companies everyone using maps is providing their location their average speed the route in which they are traveling which in turn helps Google collect massive data about the traffic which may extemporary the upcoming traffic and it adjust your route according to it which is pretty amazing right now coming to the second application which is the social media if we talk about

Facebook. one of the most common application is automatic friend tanks suggestion in Facebook and I'm sure you might have gotten this. So it's present in all the other social media platform as well. so Facebook uses face detection and image recognition to automatically find the face of the person which matches its database and hence it suggests us to tag that person based on deep face now if the face is Facebook's machine learning project which is responsible for recognition of faces and define which person is in the picture and it also provides alternative tags to the images already uploading on Facebook. for example, if we have a look at this image and we introspect the following image on Facebook we get the alt tag which has a particular description. in our case what we get here is the image may contain sky grass outdoor and nature now transportation and commuting is another industry where machine learning is used heavily. if you have used an app to book a cab recently then you are already using machine learning to an extent and what happens is that it provides a personalized application which is unique to you it automatically detects your location and provides option to either go home or office or any other frequent basis based on your history and patterns it uses a machine learning algorithm layered on top of historic trip date had to make more accurate ETA predictions now uber with the implementation of machine learning on their app and their website saw a 26 percent accuracy in delivery and pick up that's a huge a point

APPLICATIONS OF MACHINE LEARNING

Now coming to the virtual person assistant as a name suggests virtual person assistant assist in finding useful information when asked why a voice or text if you have the major applications of machine learning here a speech recognition speech to text conversion natural language processing and text-to-speech conversion all you need to do is ask a simple question like what is my schedule for tomorrow or show my upcoming flights now for answering your personal assistant searches for information or recalls your related queries to collect the information recently personal assistants are being used in chat pods which are being implemented in various food ordering apps online training web sites and also in commuting apps as well again product recommendation now this is one of the areas where machine learning is absolutely necessary and it was one of the few areas which emerged the need for machine learning now suppose you check an item on Amazon but you do not buy it then and there but the next day you are watching videos on YouTube. Suddenly you see an ad for the same item you switch to Facebook there also you see the same ad. again you go back to any other side and you see the ad for the same sort of items. So how does this happen well this happens because Google tracks your search history. recommends asked based on your search history this is one of the coolest application of machine learning and in fact, 35% of Amazon's revenue is generated by the products recommendation now coming to the cool. the highly technological side of machine learning we have self-driving cars if we talk about the self-driving car it's here. people are already using it now machine learning plays a very important role in self-driving cars as I'm sure you guys might have heard about Tesla the leader in this business. the excurrent artificial intelligence is driven by the hardware manufacturer Nvidia which is based on unsupervised learning algorithm which is a type of machine learning algorithm now in the media state that they did not train their model to detect people or any of the objects as such the model works on deep learning. Traut sources its data from the other vehicles and drivers it uses a lot of sensors which are a part of IOT. according to the data gathered by McKenzie, the automotive data will hold a tremendous value of 750 billion dollars but that's a lot of dollars we are talking about it now next again we have Google Translate now remember the time when you travel to the new place. you find it difficult to communicate with the locals or finding local spots where everything is written in different languages well those days are gone Google's G . MT which is the Google neural machine translation is a neural machine learning that works on thousands of languages and dictionary it uses natural language processing to provide the most accurate translation of any sentence of words since the tone of the word also matters it uses other techniques like POS tagging named entity recognition . chunking. it is one of the most used applications of machine learning now if we talk about dynamic pricing setting the rice price for a good or a service is an old problem in economic theory there are a vast amount of pricing strategies that depend on the objective sort be it a movie ticket a plane ticket or a cafe everything is dynamically priced now in recent year machine learning has enabled pricing solution to track buying trends and determine more competitive product prices now if we talk about uber how does Oberer determine the price of your right who was the biggest use of machine learning comes in the form of surge pricing a machine learning model named as geosearch if you are getting late for a meeting . you need to book an uber in a crowded area get ready to pay twice the normal fear even for flats if you're traveling in the festive season the chances are that prices will be twice as much as the original price now coming to the final application of machine learning we have is the online video streaming we have Netflix Hulu . Amazon Prime video now here I'm going to explain the application using the Netflix example. So with over 100 million subscribers there is no doubt that Netflix is the daddy of the online streaming world when Netflix PD dries has all the movie industrialists taken aback forcing them to us how on earth could one single website take on Hollywood now the answer is machine learning the Netflix algorithm constantly gathers massive amounts of data about user activities like when you pause rewind fast-forward what do you want the content TV shows on weekdays movies on weekend the date you watch the time you watch whenever you pause . leave content. So that if you ever come back they would such as the same video the rating events which are about four million per day the searches which are about three million per day the browsing. the scrolling behavior and a lot more now they collect this data for each subscriber they have and use the recommender system . a lot of machine learning applications and that is why they have such a huge customer retention rate. So I hope these applications are enough for you to understand how exactly machine learning is changing the way we are interacting with society. how fast it is affecting the world in which we live.

MARKET TREND: MACHINE LEARNING

So if you have a look at the market trend of the machine learning here. So as you can see initially it wasn't much in the market but if you have a look at the 2016 side there was an enormous growth in machine learning.

MARKET TREND: MACHINE LEARNING

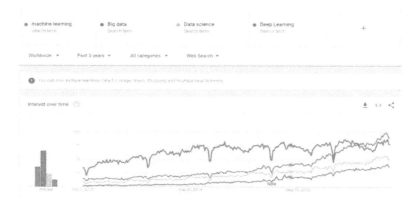

This happened mostly because you know earlier we had the idea of machine learning but then again we did not have the amount of big data. So as you can see the red line we have here in the histogram. the power plot is that of the Big Data. Big Data also increased during the years and which led to the increase in the amount of data generated . recently we had that power or I should say the underlying technology and the hardware to support that power that makes us create machine learning programs that will work on the spectator. that is why you see very high inclination during the 2016 period time as compared to 2012. So because during 2016 we got new hardware.

MARKET TREND: MACHINE LEARNING

We were able to find insights using that hardware and program and create models which would work on heavy data now let's have a look at the life cycle of machine learning. a typical machine learning life cycle has six steps. the first step is collecting data second is video wrangling then we have the third stepper be analyzed the data fourth step where we train the algorithm the fifth step is when we test the algorithm. the sixth step is when we deploy that particular algorithm for industrial uses. So when we talk about the fourth step which is collecting data.

STEP 1: COLLECTING DATA

DATA WRANGLING

Here data is being collected from various sources. this stage involves the collection of all the relevant data from various sources now if we talk about data wrangling. data wrangling is the process of cleaning and converting raw data into a format that allows convenient consumption now this is a very important part in the machine learning lifecycle as it's not every time that we receive a data which is clean . is in a proper format sometimes their value is missing sometimes there are wrong values sometimes data format is different. a major part in a machinery lifecycle goes in data wrangling and data cleaning.

ANALSE DATA

If we talk about the next step which is data analysis. data is analyzed to select and filter the data required to prepare the model. in this step, we take the data to use machine learning algorithms to create a particular model.

TRAIN ALGORITHM

Now next again when we have a model what we do is strain the model now here we use the data sets. the algorithm is trained on between data set through which algorithm understand the pattern and the rules which govern the particular data once we have trained the algorithm next comes testing.

TEST ALGORITHM

The testing data set determines the accuracy of our models. what we do is provide the test dataset to the model. which tells us the accuracy of the particular model whether it's 60% 70% 80% depending upon the requirement of the company and finally we have the operation and optimization.

OPERATION AND OPTIMIZATION

If the speed and accuracy of the model is acceptable then that moral should be deployed in the real system the model that is used in the production should be made with all the available data models improve with the amount of available data used to create them all the result of the moral needs to be incorporated in the business strategy now after the model is deployed based upon its performance the model is updated and improved if there is a dip in the performance the moral is retrained. all of these happen in the operation and optimization stage now before we move forward since machine learning is mostly done in Python and us. and if we have a look at the difference between Python and our I'm pretty sure most of the people would go for Python. the major reason why people go for python is that python has a number of libraries and python is being used in just more than data analysis and machine learning.

IMPORTANT PYTHON LIBRARIES

Some of the important Python libraries here which I want to discuss here. first of all, I'll talk about matplotlib now what Matt brought lib does is that it enables you to make bar charts scatter plots the line charts histogram basically what it does is helps in the visualization aspect as a data analyst. machine learning ingenious what one needs to represent the data in such a format that it is used that it can be understood by non-technical people such as people from marketing people from sales and other departments as well.

IMPORTANT PYTHON LIBRARIES

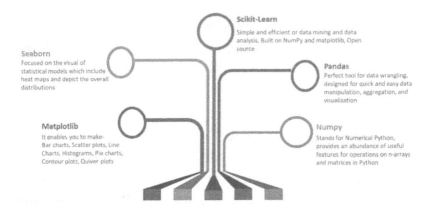

Scikit-Learn
Simple and efficient or data mining and data analysis, Built on NumPy and matplotlib, Open source

Seaborn
Focused on the visual of statistical models which include heat maps and depict the overall distributions

Pandas
Perfect tool for data wrangling, designed for quick and easy data manipulation, aggregation, and visualization

Matplotlib
It enables you to make- Bar charts, Scatter plots, Line Charts, Histograms, Pie charts, Contour plots, Quiver plots

Numpy
Stands for Numerical Python, provides an abundance of useful features for operations on n-arrays and matrices in Python

So another important Python library here we have a seaborne which is focused on the visuals of statistical models which includes heat maps. depict the overall distributions sometimes people work on data which are more geographically aligned and I would say in those cases the traps are very much required now next we come to scikit-learn and sci-kit-learn is one of the most famous libraries of python I would say it's simple and efficient or data mining . for data analysis it is built on numpy and my rock lab and it is open-source next on our list we have pandas it is the perfect tool for data wrangling which is designed for quick . easy data manipulation aggregation and visualization and finally we have numpy now numpy stands for a numerical Python provides an abundance of useful features for operation on n arrays which has an umpire's. matrices in spite and mostly it is used for mathematical purposes. So which gives a plus point to any machine learning algorithm. as these were the important part in larry's which one must know in order to do any price and programming for machine learning or as such if you are doing Python programming you need to know about all of these libraries.

TYPES OF MACHINE LEARNING

Guys next what we are going to discuss other types of machine learning. So then again we have three types of machine learning which are supervised reinforcement.

TYPES OF MACHINE LEARNING

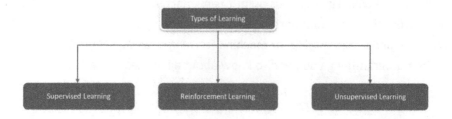

unsupervised machine learning.

SUPERVISED LEARNING

If we talk about supervised machine learning so supervised learning is where you have the input variable X and the output variable Y and you use an also I know to learn the mapping function from the input to the output. if we take the case of object detection here so or face detection I rather say. first of all, what we do is input the raw data in the form of labeled faces and again it's not necessary that we just input faces to train the model what we do is input a mixture of faces. non-faces images.

SUPERVISED LEARING

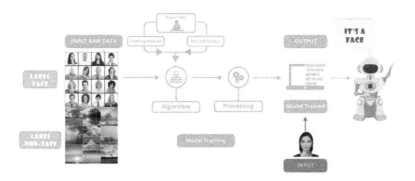

As you can see here we have labeled face and labeled on faces what we do is provide the data to the algorithm the algorithm creates a model it uses the training dataset to understand what exactly is in a face what exactly is in a picture which is not a face . after the model is done with the training and processing. to test it what we do is provide a particular input of a face or an on face what we now see the major part of supervised learning here is that we exactly know the output. when we are providing a face we our selves know that it's a phase. to test that particular model and get the accuracy we use the labeled input raw data.

UNSUPERVISED LEARNING

Next when we talk about unsupervised learning unsupervised learning is the training of a model using information that is neither classified nor labeled now this model can be used to cluster the input data in classes or the basis of the statistical properties for example for a basket full of vegetables we can cluster different vegetables based upon their color or sizes. if I have a look at this particular example here we have what we are doing is we are inputting the raw data which can be either apple banana or mango what we don't have here which was previously there in supervised learning are the labels. what the algorithm does is that it visually gets the features of a particular set of data it makes clusters. what will happen is that it will make a cluster of red looking fruits which are Apple yellow local fruits which are banana. based upon the shape also it determines what exactly the fruit is. categorizes it as mango banana or apple. this is unsupervised learning now the third type of learning which we have here is reinforcement learning.

REINFORCEMENT LEARNING

So reinforcement learning is the learning by interacting with space or an environment it selects the action on the basis of its past experience the exploration . also by new choices, a reinforcement learning agent learns from the consequences of its action rather than from being taught explicitly. So if we have a look at the example where the input data we have what it does is goes to the training goes to the agent where the agent selects the algorithm it takes the best action from the environment gets the reward and the model is strange.

REINFORCEMENT LEARNING

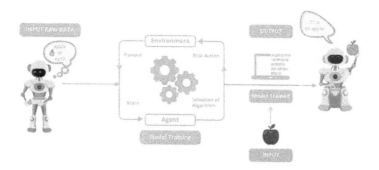

If you provide a picture of a green apple although the Apple which it particularly nose is read what it will do is it will try to get an answer . with the past experience what it has and it will recreate the algorithm and then finally provide an output which is according to our requirements. now, these were the major types of machine learning algorithms next what we never do is dig deep into all of these types of machine learning one by one. let's get started with supervised learning first. understand what exactly is supervised learning and what are the different algorithms inside it how it works the algorithms the working. we'll have a look at the various algorithm demos now which will make you understand it in a much better way.

SUPERVISED LEARNING

let's go ahead and understand what exactly is supervised learning. supervised learning is where you have the input variable X. the output variable Y and using an algorithm to learn the mapping function from the input to the output as I mentioned earlier with the example of face detection. it is cos Subbu is learning because the process of an algorithm learning from the training data set can be thought of as a teacher supervising the learning process. if we have a look at the supervised learning steps or what will rather say the workflow.

SUPERVISED LEARNING

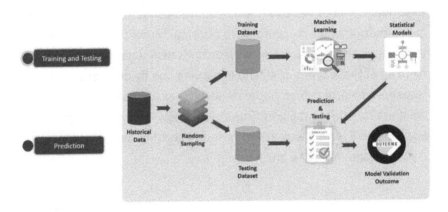

The model is used as you can see here we have the historical data then we again we have the random sampling we split the data enter training error set . the testing data set using the training data set we with the help of machine learning which is supervised machine learning we create statistical model now after we have a model which is being generated with the help of the training data set what we do is use the testing data set for prediction and testing what we do is get the output.

SUPERVISED LEARNING

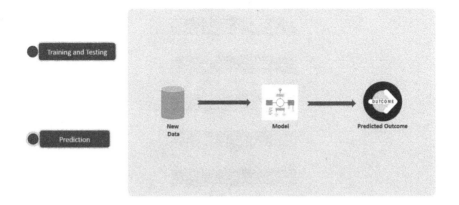

Finally, if we have the model validation outcome that was third training and testing. if we have a look at the prediction part of any particular supervised learning algorithm. the model is used for operating outcome of a new data set. So whenever the performance of the model degraded the model is retrained or if there are any performance issues the model is retrained with the help of the new data now when we talk about a supervisor in there are not just one but quite a few algorithms here.

SUPERVISED LEARNING ALGORITHMS

So we have linear regression logistic regression this is entry we have random forest we have made biased classifiers. linear regression is used to estimate real values for the cost of houses the number of cars the total sales based on the continuous variable. that is what Rainier generation is now when we talk about logistic regression it is used to estimate discrete values for example which are binary values like zero and one yes or no true and false based on the given set of independent way. for example when you are talking about something like the chance of winning or if we talk about winning which can be true or false if will it rain today which it can be the yes or no.

43

SUPERVISED LEARNING ALGORITHMS

It cannot be like when the output of a particular algorithm or the particular question is either yes/no or binary then only we use a logic regression now next we have decision trees. these are used for classification problems it works for both categorical. continuous dependent variables and if we talk over the random forest. random forest is an N symbol of a decision tree it gives better prediction and accuracy that decision tree. that is another type of supervised learning algorithm and finally, we have the Nate Byars classifier. it is a classification technique based on the based theorem with an assumption of independence between predictors. we'll get more into the details of all of these algorithms one by one so let's get started with linear regression.

LINEAR REGRESSION

First of all, let us understand what exactly linear regression is. linear regression analysis is a powerful technique you operating the unknown value of a variable which is the dependent variable from the known value of another variable which is the independent variable.

LINEAR REGRESSION

Linear Regression Analysis is a powerful technique used for predicting the unknown value of a variable (**Dependent Variable**) from the known value of another variables (**Independent Variable**)

- A Dependent Variable(DV) is the variable to be predicted or explained in a regression model
- An Independent Variable(IDV) is the variable related to the dependent variable in a regression equation

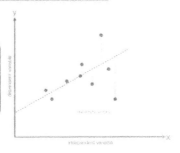

A dependent variable is a variable to be predicted or explained in a regression model whereas an independent variable is a variable related to the dependent variable in a regression equation.

SIMPLE LINEAR REGRESSION

So if you have a look here as a simple linear regression. So it's basically equivalent to a simple line which is with a slope which is y equals a plus B X where Y is the dependent variable a is the y-intercept we have P which is the slope of the line. X which is the independent variable. intercept is the value of the dependent variable Y when the value of the independent variable X is 0 it is the the line cuts the y-axis whereas slope is the change in the dependent variable for a unit increase in the independent variable it is the tangent of the angle made by the line with the x-axis now when we talk about the relation between the variables we have a particular term which is known as correlation.

SIMPLE LINEAR REGRESSION

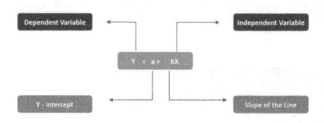

Correlation is an important factor to check the dependencies when there are multiple variables what it does is it gives us an insight of the mutual relationship among variables and it is used for creating a correlation plot with the help of the Seabourn library which I mentioned earlier which is one of the most important libraries in Python.

REGRESSION LINE

Correlation is a very important term to know about now if we talk about regression lines. So linear regression analysis is a powerful technique used for predicting the unknown value of a variable which is the dependent variable from the regression line which is simply a single line that best fits the data in terms of having the smallest overall distance from the line to the points.

REGRESSION LINE

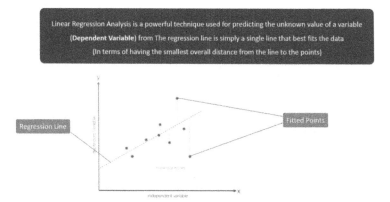

So as you can see in the plot here we have the different points or the data point. these are known as the fitted points then again we have the regression line which has the smallest overall distance from the line to the points. you have a look at the distance between the point to the regression line. So what this line shows is the deviation from the regression line. So exactly how far the point is from the regression line. So let's understand a simple use case of linear regression with the help of a demo.

REAL ESTATE COMPANY USE CASE

First of all, there is a real state company use case which I'm going to talk about. first of all, here we have John he has some baseline for pricing the villas and the independent houses he has in Boston. So here we have the data set description which we're going to use.

DATASET DESCRIPTION

So this data set has different columns such as the crime rate per capita which is CRIM it has proportional residential. zone for the Lots proportion of non-retail business the river the United Rock side concentration average number of rooms and the proportion of the owner occupying the built prior to 1940 the distance of the five Boston employment centers in excess of accessibility to Riedl highways and much more. first of all, let's have a look at the data set we have here.

DATASET DESCRIPTION

Column	Description
CRIM	per capita crime rate by town
ZN	proportion of residential land zoned for lots over 25,000 sq.ft.
INDUS	proportion of non-retail business acres per town.
CHAS	Charles River dummy variable (1 if tract bounds river; 0 otherwise)
NOX	nitric oxides concentration (parts per 10 million)
RM	average number of rooms per dwelling
AGE	proportion of owner-occupied units built prior to 1940
DIS	weighted distances to five Boston employment centres
RAD	index of accessibility to radial highways
TAX	full-value property-tax rate per $10,000
PTRATIO	pupil-teacher ratio by town
B	1000(Bk - 0.63)^2 where Bk is the proportion of blacks by town
LSTAT	% lower status of the population
MEDV	Median value of owner-occupied homes in $1000's

one number I don't think here guys is that I'm gonna be using Jupiter notebook to execute all my practicals you are free to use the spider notebook or the console either. it basically comes down to your preference. for my preference I'm going to use the Jupiter notebook. for this use case, we're gonna use the Boston housing data set. as you can see here we have the data set which has the CRI min in desc CAS NO x the different variables. We have the data set of form almost I would say like 500 houses. what John needs to do is plan the pricing of the housing depending upon all of these different variables. that it's profitable for him to sell the house and it's easier for the customers also to buy the house. first of all, let me open the code here for you so first of all what we're gonna do is import the library is necessary for this project. So we're going to use the number we're going to import numpy as NP import pandas at PD then we're gonna also import the matplotlib and then we are going to do is read the Boston housing data set into the BOS one variable. now what we are going to do is create two variables x andy.

What we're gonna do is take 0 to 13 I'll say is from CR I am two LS data in 1x because that's the independent variable. Y here is a dependent variable which is the MA TV which is the final price. So first of all what we need to do is plot a correlation. what we're gonna do is import the Seabourn library as SN s we're going to use the correlations to plot the correlations between the different 0 to 13 variables what we gonna do is also use ma DV here also. what we're going to do is SN s dot heatmap correlations to be going to use the square to differentiate usually it comes up in square only or circles. you don't know so we're gonna use square you want to see you see the map with the Y as GNP you this is the color. So there's no rotation in the y-axis and we're gonna rotate the excesses to the 90 degrees and lets we gonna plot it now. this is what the plot looks like. So as you can see here the thicker or the darker the color gets the more is the correlation between the variables. for example, if you have a look at CRIM. M a DV right. as you can see here the color is very less where the correlation is very low. one thing important what we can see here is the tax and our ad which is the full value of the property and RIT is the index of accessibility to the radial highways now these things are highly correlated. that is natural because the more it is connected to the highway and closer it is to the highway the easier it is for people to travel and hence the tax on it is more as it is closer to the highways now what we're going to do it from SQL. dot cross-validation we're going to import the Train test split and we're gonna split the data set now. So what we're going to do is create four variables which are the extreme X test Y train white tests and we're going to use a training test split function to split the x andy and here we're going to use the test size 0.3 tree which will split the data set into the test size will be 33% well as the training size will be 67% now this is dependent on you usually it is either 60/40 70/30 this depends on your use case your data you have the kind of output you are getting the model you are creating . much more than again from SQL learn dot linear model we're going to import linear regression now this is the major functions we're gonna use just linear regression function which is present in SQL which is a scikit-learn. So we going to create our linear regression model into LM and the model which are going to create and we're going to fit the training videos which has the X train and the why train then we're gonna create a prediction underscore 5 which is the LM dot credit and I take the X test variables which will provide the predicted Y variables. So now finally if we plot the scatter plot of the Y test and they predicted what we can see is that. we give the X label as a white test and the Y label has y predicted we can see the regression line which we have plotted in at the scatter plot. if you want to draw a regression line it's usually it will go through all of these points excluding the extremities which are here present at the endpoints. So this is how a normal linear regression works in Python what you do is create a correlation you find out you split the dataset into training. testing variables then again you define what is going to be your test size import the reintegration moral use the training data set into the model fitted use the test data set to create the predictions. then use the wireless code test and the predicted Y and plot the scatter plot and see how close your model is doing with the original data it had.

STEPS

Check the accuracy of that model now typically you use these steps which were collecting data what we did data wrangling analyze the data we trained the algorithm we use the test algorithm. then we deployed. So fitting a model means that you are making your algorithm learn the relationship between predictors. the outcomes. So that you can predict the future values of the outcome. So the best fitted model has a specific set of parameters which best defines the problem at hand since this is a linear model with the equation y equals MX plus C. So in this case, the parameters of the model learns from the data that are M and C. So this is what more fitting now if it has a look at the types of fitting which are available. So first of all machine learning algorithm first attempt to Solve the problem of underfitting that is of taking a line that does not approximate the data well. making it approximate to the data better.

MODEL FITTING

So machine does not know where to stop in order to solve the problem and it can go ahead from appropriate to overfit more sometimes when we say a model overfits we mean that it may have a low error rate for training data but it may not generalize well to the overall population of the data we are interested in.

TYPES OF FITTING

TYPES OF FITTING

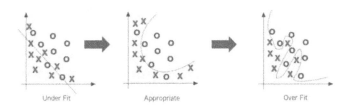

So we have under fact appropriate . over fit these are the types of fitting now guys this was linear regression which is a type of supervised learning algorithm in machine learning.

NEED FOR LOGISTIC REGRESSION

So next what we're going to do is understand the need for logistic regression. let's consider a use case as in political elections is being contested in our country. suppose that we are interested to know which candidate will probably win now the outcome variables result in binary either win or lose the predictor variables are the amount of money spent the age the popularity rank and etc etcetera nowhere the best fit line in the regression war is going below 0. above what and since the value of y will be discrete that is between 0 & 1 the linear rain has to be clipped at 0 & 1 now linear regression gives us only a single line to classify the output with linear regression our resulting curve cannot be formulated into a single formula as you obtain three different straight lines what we need is a new way to solve this problem. So hence people came up with logistic regression.

WHAT IS LOGISTIC REGRESSION?

So let's understand what exactly is logic regression So logistic regression is a statistical method for analyzing a data set in which there are 1 or more independent variables that determine an outcome. the outcome is a binary class type.

So example a patient goes a followed a teen checkup in the hospital and his interest is to know whether the cancer is benign or malignant now a patient's data such as sugar level blood pressure eight skin width. the previous medical history is recorded and a daughter checks the patient data and it reminds the outcome of his illness. severity of illness the outcome will result in binary that is zero if the cancer is malignant and one if it's been I know no strict regression is a statistical method used for analyzing a dataset there were say one or more dependent variables like we discuss like the sugar level blood pressure skin with the previous medical history and the output is binary class type. So now let's have a look at the lowest it regression curve now the law disintegration code is also called a sigmoid curve or the S curve the sigmoid function converts any value from minus infinity to infinity to the discrete value 0 or 1 now how to decide whether the value is 0 or 1 from this curve. So let's take an example what we do is provide a threshold value we set it we decide the output from that function. So let's take an example with the threshold value of 0.4. So any value above 0.4 will be rounded off to 1. anyone below 0.4 we really reduce to 0.

WHAT IS POLYNOMIAL REGRESSION?

So similarly, we have polynomial regression also so when we have nonlinear data which cannot be predicted with a linear model we switch to the polynomial regression now such a scenario is shown in the below graph. So as you can see here we have the equation y equals 3x cubed plus 4x squared minus 5x plus 2 now here we cannot perform this linearly. So we need polynomial regression to solve these kinds of problems now when we talk about logistic regression there is an important term which is decision tree.

WHAT IS DECISION TREE?

This is one of the most used algorithms in supervised learning now let's understand what exactly is a decision tree. So our decision tree is a tree-like structure in which internal load represents tests on an attribute now each attribute represents the outcome of a test.

WHAT IS A DECISION TREE?

A decision tree is a tree-like structure in which internal node represents test on an attribute

- Each branch represents outcome of test and each leaf node represents class label (decision taken after computing all attributes)

- A path from root to leaf represents classification rules.

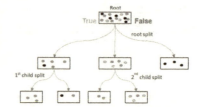

Each leaf node represents the class label which is a decision taken after computing all attributes apart from root to the leaf represents classification rules. a decision tree is made from our data by analyzing the variables from the decision tree now from the tree we can easily find out whether there will become tomorrow if the conditions are rainy. less windy now let's see how we can implement the same.

BUILDING A DECISION TREE

So suppose here we have a data set in which we have the outlook. So what we can do is from each of the Outlawz we can divide the data as sunny overcast and rainy. So as you can see on the sunny side we get two yeses. three noes because the outlook is sunny the humidity is now the oven is weak and strong. So it's a fully sunny day what we have is that it's not a pure subset. So what we're gonna do is split it further. So if you have a look at the overcast we have humidity high normal week. So yes during overcast weekend play. if you have a look at the Raney's area we have three SS and − no. So again what we're going to do is split it further.

BUILDING A DECISION TREE

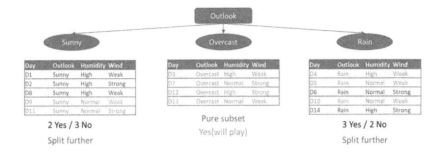

So when we talk of a sunny then we have humidity in humidity we have high and normal.

BUILDING A DECISION TREE

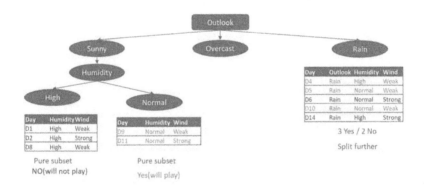

So when the humidity is normal we're going to play which is the pure subset and if the humidity is high we are not going to play which is also a pure subset now. So let's do the same for the rainy day. So during the rainy day, we have the vent classifier.

BUILDING A DECISION TREE

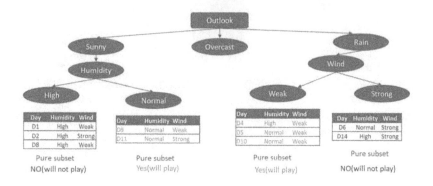

So if the wind is to be it becomes a pure subset we're going to play and if the vent is strong it's a pure substance we not gonna play.the final decision tree looks like this.

BUILDING A DECISION TREE

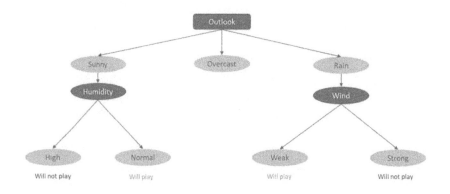

So first of all we check if the outlook is sunny overcast or rain if it's overcast we will play if it's sunny we then again check the humidity if the humidity is high we will not play if the humidity is normal real play then again in the case of rainy if we check the vent if the wind is weak the play will go on and similarly if the wind is strong the play must stop. this is how exactly a decision tree works. So let's go ahead. see how we can implement logistics relation in decision trees now for logistic regression we're going to use the Casa data set.

jupyter Logistic Regression - DTrees Last Checkpoint: 21 hours ago (autosaved)   Logout

File   Edit   View   Insert   Cell   Kernel   Widgets   Help   Not Trusted   Python 3 O

```
In [1]: from sklearn.model_selection import cross_val_score
        import numpy as np # linear algebra
        import pandas as pd # data processing, CSV file I/O (e.g. pd.read_csv), data manipulation as in SQL
        import matplotlib.pyplot as plt # this is used for the plot the graph
        import seaborn as sns # used for plot interactive graph. I like most for plot
        from sklearn.linear_model import LogisticRegression # to apply the logistic regression
        from sklearn.model_selection import train_test_split # to split the data into two parts
        from sklearn import metrics # for the check the error and accuracy of the model
        from sklearn.tree import DecisionTreeClassifier
        # Any results you write to the current directory are saved as output.
        # dont worry about the error if its not working then insteda of model_selection we can use cross_validation
```

```
In [3]: data = pd.read_csv("data.csv",header=0)
        # here header 0 means the 0 th row is our coloumn name
        # have a look at the data
        print(data.head(6))# as u can see our data have imported and having 33 columns
        # head is used for to see top 5 by default I used 2 so it will print 6 rows
        # now lets look at the type of data we have. We can use
        data.info()
```

```
         id diagnosis  radius_mean  texture_mean  perimeter_mean  area_mean \
0    842302         M        17.99         10.38          122.80    1001.0
1    842517         M        20.57         17.77          132.90    1326.0
2  84300903         M        19.69         21.25          130.00    1203.0
3  84348301         M        11.42         20.38           77.58     386.1
4  84358402         M        20.29         14.34          135.10    1297.0
5    843786         M        12.45         15.70           82.57     477.1

   smoothness_mean  compactness_mean  concavity_mean  concave points_mean \
```

this is how the data set looks like So here we have the eye diagnosis radius mean - I mean parameter means these are the stats of particular cancer cells or the cyst which are present in the body. So we have like total 33 columns all the way starting from IDE - unnamed 32. So our main goal here is to define whether or I'll say predict whether the cancer is pining on the mannequin. first of all, what vinegar - is from scikit-learn dot small selection we're gonna import cross-validation score and again we're going to use numpy for linear algebra we're gonna use pandas as PD because for data processing the CSV file input for data manipulation in a sequel. most of the stuff then we're going to import the matplotlib it is used for plotting the graph we're going to import Seabourn which is used to plot interactive graph like in the last example we saw we plotted a heatmap correlation. So from SK learn we're going to import the logistic regression which is the major model or the algorithm behind the whole logic regression we're gonna import the train dressed split. So as to split the raita into two paths training. testing data set we're going to import metrics to check the error and the accuracy of the model and we're gonna import decision tree classifier. So first of all what we're gonna do is create a variable data. use the pandas PD to read the data from the data set. So here the header 0 means that the zeroth row is our column name and if we have a look at the data or the top six part of the data we're going to use the friend data dot head . get the data dot info. So as you can see here we have. So many data columns such as highly diagnosis radius being in the text remain parameter main area means smoothness mean we have texture worst symmetry worst we have fractal dimension worse. lastly, we have the unnamed. So, first of all, we can see we have six rows and 33 columns and if you have a look at all of these columns here right we get the total number which is the 569 which is the total number of observation we have. we check whether it's not null and then again we check the type of the particular column. So it's integer it's object float mostly most of them are float Some is an integer.

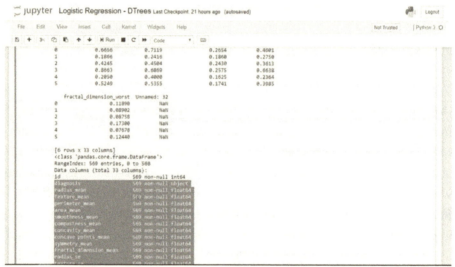

So now again we're going to drop the unnamed column which is the column 30 second 0 to 33 which is the 30-second column. So in this process, we will change it in our data itself. So if you want to save the old data you can also see if that but then again that's of no use. So theta dot columns will give us all of these columns when we remove that. So you can see here in the output we do not have the final one which was the unnamed the last one we have is the type which is a float. So latex we also don't want the ID column for our analysis. So what we're gonna do is we're gonna drop the ID again. So as I said above the data can be divided into three paths. let's divide the features according to their category now as you know our diagnosis column is object type. we can map it to the integer value. So we what we wanna do is use the data diagnosis and we're gonna map it to M 1 and B 0. So that the output is either M or B now if we use a rated or described. So you can see here we have 8 rows and 1 column because we dropped two of the columns and in the diagonals, we have the values here let's get the frequency of the cancer stages. So here we're going to use the Seabourn SNS not count plot data with diagnosis and Lee will come and if we use the PLT dot show. So here you can see the diagnosis for 0 is more and for 1 is less if you plot the correlation among this data. So we're going to use the PLT dot figure SNS start heat map we're gonna use a heat map we're going to plot the correlation c by true we're going to use square true. we're gonna use the cold warm technique. So as you can see here the correlation of the radius worst with the area worst and the parameter worst is more whereas the radius worst has a high correlation to the parameter mean and the area mean because if the radius is more the parameter is more area is more. So based on the core plot let's select some features from the model now the decision is made in order to remove the: era t so we will have a prediction variable in which we have the texture mean the parameter means the smoothness means the compactors mean. the symmetry means but these are the variables which we'll use for the prediction now we'll gonna split the data into the training and testing data set now in this our main data is split into training a test data set with the 0.3 test size that is 30 to 70 ratio next what we're going to do is check the dimension of that training . the testing data says. So what we're going to do is use the print command and pass the parameter train dot shape test our shape. So what we can see here is that we have almost like 400 398 observations were 31 columns in the training dataset whereas 171 rows and 31 columns in the testing dataset. So then again what we're going to do is take the training data input what we're going to do is create a Train underscore X with the prediction underscore rad and train is for y is for the diagnosis now this is the output of our training data same as we did for the test. So we're going to use test underscore X for the test prediction variable. test underscore Y for the test diagnosis which is the output of the test data now we're going to create a logistic regression method. create a model logistic dot fit in which you're going to fit the training data set which is strain X entering Y and then we're going to use a TEMP which is a temporary variable in which you can operate X and then what we're going to do is we're going to compare to EMP which is a test X with the test Y to check the accuracy. So the accuracy here we get is 0.9 1 then again what we need to do this was like location normal roads retribution are we going to use the classifier. So we're going to create a decision tree classifier with the random state given as 0 now what next we're going to do is create the cross-validation school which is the CLF we take the moral we take the train X 3. Y and CV equal 10 the cross-validation score now if we fit the training test and the sample weight we have not defined here check the input of his true and XID x sorted is none. So if we get the parameters true we predict using the test X. then predict the long probability of test X and if we compare the score of test X to test Y with the sample weight none we get the same result as a decision tree. So this is how you implement a decision tree classifier. check the accuracy of the particular model. So that was it.

WHAT IS RANDOM FOREST?

So next on our list is random forest so let's understand what exactly is a random forest. random forest is a symbol classifier made using many decision tree models.

WHAT IS RANDOM FOREST

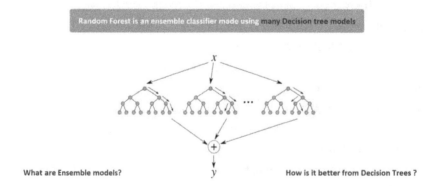

Random Forest is an ensemble classifier made using many Decision tree models

x

What are Ensemble models? y How is it better from Decision Trees ?

So what exactly are in symbol malls. son symbol malls combine the results from different models the result from an N simple mall is usually better than the result of the one of the individual model because every tree votes for one class the final decision is based upon the majority of votes and it is better than the decision tree because compared to decision tree it can be much more accurate it rests if efficiently on the last data set it can handle thousands of input variables without variable deletion . what it does is it gives an estimate of what variables are important in the classification. So let's take the example of weather data so let's understand I know for us with the help of the hurricanes and typhoons data set. so we have the data about hurricanes and typhoons from 1851 to 2014. the data comprises off location when the pressure of tropical cyclones in the Pacific Ocean the based on the data we have to classify the storms into hurricanes typhoons.

PREDEFINED CLASS DESCRIPTION

The subcategories as further to predefined classes mentioned. So the predefined classes are TD tropical cyclone of tropical depression intensity which is less than 34 knots if it's between thirty-four to six to 18 oz it's Ds greater than 64 knots it's a cheer which is a hurricane intensity e^x is a tropical cyclone s T is less than 34 it's a subtropical cyclone or subtropical depression ss is greater than 34 which is a subtropical cyclone of subtropical storm intensity . then again we have Lo which is a low that is neither a tropical cyclone a tropical-subtropical cyclone or not an extraterrestrial cyclone and then again finally, we have DB which is a disturbance of any intensity now these were the predefined classes description.

PREDEFINED CLASS DESCRIPTION

1. TD – Tropical cyclone of tropical depression intensity (< 34 knots)

2. TS – Tropical cyclone of tropical storm intensity (34-63 knots)

3. HU – Tropical cyclone of hurricane intensity (> 64 knots)

4. EX – Extratropical cyclone (of any intensity)

5. SD – Subtropical cyclone of subtropical depression intensity (< 34 knots)

6. SS – Subtropical cyclone of subtropical storm intensity (> 34 knots)

7. LO – A low that is neither a tropical cyclone, a subtropical cyclone, nor an extratropical cyclone (of any intensity) DB – Disturbance (of any intensity)

So as you can see this is the data in which we have the ID name date event say this line it's your longitude maximum when minimum when there are. So many variables So let's start with imp the pandas then again we import the matplotlib then we gonna use the aggregate method in matplotlib we're going to use the matplotlib in line which is used for plotting interactive graph and I like it most for plots. So next what we're going to do is import Seabourn as SNS now this is used to plot the graph again. we're going to import the model selection which is the Train test split. So we're gonna import it from a scaler and the sci-kit-learn we have to import metrics watching the accuracy then we have to Import sq learn and then again from SQL. we have to import tree from SQL or dot + symbol we're gonna import the random forest classifier from SQL and Road metrics we're going to import confusion matrix. So as to check the accuracy . from SQL and on the message we're gonna also import the accuracy score. So let's import random and let's read the dataset. print the first six rows of the data sets you can see here we have the ID we have the name date time it will stay this latitude longitude. so in total, we have 22 columns here so as you can see here we have a column name status which is TS TS TS for the four six. So what we're gonna do is data at our state as visible P dot categorical data the state. So what we can do is make it a categorical data with quotes so that it's easier for the machine to understand. it rather than having certain categories as means we're gonna use the categories as numbers. So it's easier for the computer to do the analysis. so let's get the frequency of different typhoons. So what we're going to do is random dot seed then again what are we gonna do is if we have to drop the status we have to drop the event because these are unnecessary we're gonna drop latitude longitude we're gonna drop ID then name the date and the time it occurred. so if we print the prediction list so ignore the error here so that's not necessary. So we have the maximum and minimum and pressure low went any low when deci low when s top blue and these are the parameters on which we're going to do the predictions. So now we'll split that into training and testing data sets So then again we have the trained comet test. we're gonna use a trained test split especially in the 70s of 30 industrial standard ratios now an important thing here to note is that you can split it in any form you want can be either 60/40 70/30 80/20 it all depends upon the model which you have our the industrial requirement which you have. So then again if after printing let's check the dimensions. the training dataset comprises of eighteen thousand two hundred. ninety-five rows were twenty-two columns whereas the testing dataset comprised of eight thousand rows with twenty-two columns we have the training data input train x we had a train. status is the final output of the training data which will tell us the status whether it's a TS dd which it's a hu which kind of a hurricane or typhoon or any kind of subcategories which are defined which were like subtropical cyclone the subtropical typhoon and much more. So our prediction or the output variable will be status so. So this is these are the list of the training columns which we have here now same we have to do for the test variable. So we have the test x with the prediction underscore rat with a testy with the status. So now what we're going to do is build a random foils classifier. So in the model, we have the random forest classifier with estimators as 100 a simple random for small and then we fit the training data set which is a training X. train by then we again make the prediction which is the world or predict that with the test underscores X then that. this will predict for the test data and prediction will contain the rated value by our model predicted values of the diagnosis column for the test inputs. So if you print the metrics of the accuracy score between the prediction and the test. a score of why to check the accuracy we get 95% accuracy now the same if we're going to do with a decision tree. So again we're gonna use the model tree dot decision tree classifier we're going to use the Train X and tree in Y

63

which other training data sets new prediction is smaller for a task or text we're going to create a data frame which is the Parador data frame. if we have a look at the prediction and the test underscore Y you can see the state has 10 10 3 3 10 10 11 and 5 5 3 11 and 3 3. so it goes on . on so it has 7840 2 rows and 1 column and if you print the accuracy we get a ninety-five point five seven percent of accuracy . if you have a look at the accuracy of the random for us we get 95 points six percent which is more than 95 point five seven. So as I mentioned earlier usually random forest gives a better output or creates a better more than the decision tree classifier because as I mentioned earlier it combines the result from different models you know. So the final decision is based upon the majority of votes . is usually higher than the decision tree models. So let's move ahead with our knee by selca rhythm and let's see what exactly is neat bias.

WHAT IS NAÏVE BAYES?

So nave bias is a simple but surprisingly powerful algorithm for predictive modeling now it is a classification technique based on the base theorem with an assumption of independence among predictors it comprises of two parts which are the nave and the bias. So in simple terms and a bias classifier assumes that the presence of a particular feature in a class is unrelated to the presence of any other feature even of these features depend on each other or upon the existence of the other features all of these properties independently contribute to the probability that a fruit it's an apple or an orange . that is why it is known as a noun a base model is easy to build and particularly useful for very large data sets in probability theory and statistics.

BAYES' THEOREM

Bayes theorem which is alternatively known as the base law or the Bayes rule also emitted as Bayes theorem describes the probability of an event based on the prior knowledge of conditions that might be related to the event.

So Bayes theorem is a way to figure out the conditional probability now conditional probability is the probability of an event happening given that it has some to one or more other events, for example, your probability of getting a parking space is connected to the town today you park where you park. what conventions are going on at the same time? So base Hyrum is slightly more nuanced. a nutshell it gives us the actual probability of an event given information about tests. So let's talk about the base Hyrum now so now given any I policies edge. evidence II Bayes theorem states that the relationship between the probability of the hypothesis before getting the evidence pH and the probability of the hypothesis after getting the evidence which is PH bare is PE bar H into probability of H there are a probability of e which means it's the probability of even after in the hypothesis inter priority of the hypothesis divided by the probability of the evidence.

BAYES' THEOREM EXAMPLE

So let's understand it with a simple example here. So now for example if a single card is drawn from standard deck of playing cards the probability of that card being a king is 4 out of 52 now since there are 4 kings in a standard deck of 52 cards the rewarding this if the king is the event this card is a king the priority of the king that is the probability of king equals 4 by 52 which in turn is 1 by 30 now if the event is

BAYE'S THEOREM EXAMPLE

$$P(A|B) = \frac{P(A \cap B)}{P(B)}$$

$$P(B|A) = \frac{P(B \cap A)}{P(A)}$$

$$P(A \cap B) = P(A|B).P(B) = P(B|A).P(A)$$

$$= P(A|B) = \frac{P(B|A).P(A)}{P(B)}$$

is varieties or instance someone looks at the card that the single card is a face card then the posterior probability which is the P of King given it's a face can be calculated using the Bayes theorem given the probability of King given its face is equal to probability of the face given its a king there is a probability of face into the probability of King since every King is also a face card. So the probability of face given its a king is equal to 1. since there are 3 face cards in each suit that are jacking and Queen the probability of face card is 3 out of 30 combining these given likelihood ratios are we get the value using. the paste theorem of the probability of King events of the face is equal to 1 out of 3 so foreign joint probability distribution with events a. B the probability of an intersection B which is the conditional probability of a given B is now defined as the property of intersection B divided by the probability of B now this is how we get the base theorem now that we know the different basic proof of how we got the base theorem. So let's have a look at the working of the base your answer with the help of examples here.

CLASSIFICATION STEPS

So let's take the same example of the radius set of these forecasts in which we had the sunny rainy overcast. So first of all what we're gonna do is first we will create a frequency table using each attribute of the data set.

CLASSIFICATION STEPS

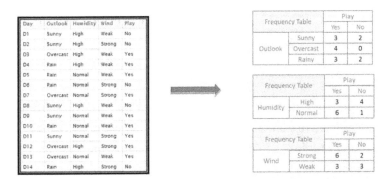

So as you can see here we have the frequency table here for the outlook humidity. the wind So for Outlook we have the frequency table here we have the frequency table for humidity and the wind. So next what we're gonna do is create the probability of sunny given say s that is three out of ten find the probability of sunny which is five out of 14.

CLASSIFICATION STEPS

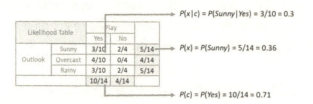

$P(x|c) = P(Sunny|Yes) = 3/10 = 0.3$

Likelihood Table		Play		
		Yes	No	
	Sunny	3/10	2/4	5/14
Outlook	Overcast	4/10	0/4	4/14
	Rainy	3/10	2/4	5/14
		10/14	4/14	

$P(x) = P(Sunny) = 5/14 = 0.36$

$P(c) = P(Yes) = 10/14 = 0.71$

Likelihood of 'Yes' given Sunny is

$P(c|x) = P(Yes|Sunny) = P(Sunny|Yes)* P(Yes) / P(Sunny) = (0.3 \times 0.71) /0.36 = 0.591$

Similarly Likelihood of 'No' given Sunny is

$P(c|x) = P(No|Sunny) = P(Sunny|No)* P(No) / P(Sunny) = (0.4 \times 0.36) /0.36 = 0.40$

This 14 comes from the total number of observations there and from yes and no. So similarly we're gonna find the probability of yes also which is 10 out of 14 which is 0.7 one for each frequency table will generate this kind of likelihood tables. So the likelihood of yes given it's sunny is equal to 0.51 similarly the likelihood of no given sunny is equal to 0.40. So here you can look that using Bayes theorem we have found out the likelihood of yes given it's sunny. no given it's a sunny similarly we're gonna do the save all likelihood table for humidity and the same for wind.

CLASSIFICATION STEPS

Likelihood table for Humidity

Likelihood Table		Play		
		Yes	No	
Humidity	High	3/9	4/5	7/14
	Normal	6/9	1/5	7/14
		9/14	5/14	

$P(Yes|High) = 0.33 \times 0.6 / 0.5 = 0.42$

$P(No|High) = 0.8 \times 0.36 / 0.5 = 0.58$

Likelihood table for Wind

Likelihood Table		Play		
		Yes	No	
Wind	Weak	6/9	2/5	8/14
	Strong	3/9	3/5	6/14
		9/14	5/14	

$P(Yes|Weak) = 0.67 \times 0.64 / 0.57 = 0.75$

$P(No|Weak) = 0.4 \times 0.36 / 0.57 = 0.25$

So for humidity we're gonna check the probability of yes given its high humidity is a high probability of plane no given the humidity is high is your going to calculate it using the same base theorem. So suppose we have a day with the following values in which we have the outlook as rain humidity as high and wind as we since we discussed the same example earlier with the decision tree we know the answer.

So let's not get ahead of ourselves and let's try to find out the answer using the Bayes theorem let's understand how neat bass works actually. So, first of all, we gonna use the likelihood of yes on that day. So that equals to the probability of Outlook of rain given it's a yes into the probability of humidity high given SAS interpretive NVQ NCS into the probability of yes okay. So that gives us zero point zero one nine similarly they're probably likelihood of noon that day is the outlook is rain in units and no humidity is high given its and no and win this week given.

CLASSIFICATION STEPS

Suppose we have a day with the following values

Outlook	=	Rain
Humidity	=	High
Wind	=	Weak
Play	=	?

Likelihood of 'Yes' on that Day = P(Outlook = Rain|Yes)*P(Humidity= High|Yes)* P(Wind= Weak|Yes)*P(Yes)
= 2/9 * 3/9 * 6/9 * 9/14 = 0.0199

Likelihood of 'No' on that Day = P(Outlook = Rain|No)*P(Humidity= High|No)* P(Wind= Weak|No)*P(No)
= 2/5 * 4/5 * 2/5 * 5/14 = 0.0166

So know that equals to zero point zero one six now what we're going to do is find the probability of Vs and no and for that what we're going to do is take the probability the likelihood and divide it with the sum of the likelihoods obvious and known. so and that really gonna get the probability of yes overall. So you think that formula we get the probability of years as zero points five and the probability of no as zero point four five and our model predicts that there is a fifty five percent chance that there will be game tomorrow.

INDUSTRIAL USE CASES

If it's rainy the humidity is high and the wind is weak now if you have a look at the industrial use cases of any bias we have new scatterings use categorization as what happens is that the news comes in a lot of tags and it has to be categorized. So that the user gets information he needs in a particular format then again we have spam filtering which is one of the major use cases of Nate Byars classifier as it classifies the email as spam or ham then finally we have with a prediction also as we saw just with the example that we predict whether we're going to play or not that sort of prediction is always there. So, guys, this was all about supervised learning we discussed linear regression logistic regression we discussed named pies we've discussed random forests decision tree. we understood how the random forest is better than decision tree in some cases it might be equal to decision tree but nonetheless, it's always gonna provide us a better result. So guys that were all about the supervised learning. So but before that let's go ahead. see how exactly we're gonna implement nay bias. So guys here we have another data set run or walk it's the kinematic data sets and it has been measured using the mobile sensor. So let the target were able to be Y assign all the columns after it to X using sci-kit-learn a by a small we're going to observe the accuracy generate a classification report using sci-kit-learn now we're going to repeat the model once only the acceleration values as predictors and then using only the gyro value aspirators and we're going to comment on the difference in accuracy between the two moles. So here we have a data set which is run or walk. So let me open that for you so here I was data sets run or walk. So as you can see we have the date time user name risk activity acceleration XY assertions see Cairo ex Cairo y Cairo Z.

so based on it let's see how we can implement the name by is classifier and. So first of all what we're gonna do is import pandas at speedy then we gonna import matplotlib for plotting we're gonna read the run or walk data file with pandas period or tree and a CSV let's have a look at the info. So, first of all, we see that we have 88 thousand five hundred eighty-eight rows with 11 columns. So we have the date/time username rest-activity assertion XYZ Cairo XYZ and the memory uses is send point 4 MB data. So this is how you look at the columns D F dot columns now again we're gonna split the dataset into training and testing data sets. So we're going to use the Train test flight model. So that's what we're gonna do is split it into X train X testy train by test and we're gonna split it into the size of 0.2 here. So again I am saying it depends on you what is the test size.

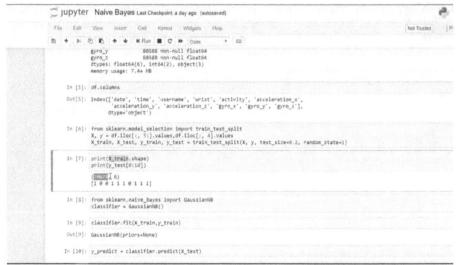

```
                gyro_y              88588 non-null float64
                gyro_z              88588 non-null float64
                dtypes: float64(6), int64(2), object(3)
                memory usage: 7.4+ MB

In [5]:  df.columns

Out[5]:  Index(['date', 'time', 'username', 'wrist', 'activity', 'acceleration_x',
                'acceleration_y', 'acceleration_z', 'gyro_x', 'gyro_y', 'gyro_z'],
                dtype='object')

In [6]:  from sklearn.model_selection import train_test_split
         X, y = df.iloc[:, 5:].values, df.iloc[:, 4].values
         X_train, X_test, y_train, y_test = train_test_split(X, y, test_size=0.2, random_state=1)

In [7]:  print(X_train.shape)
         print(y_test[0:10])

         (70870, 6)
         [1 0 0 1 1 0 1 1 1]

In [8]:  from sklearn.naive_bayes import GaussianNB
         classifier = GaussianNB()

In [9]:  classifier.fit(X_train,y_train)

Out[9]:  GaussianNB(priors=None)

In [10]: y_predict = classifier.predict(X_test)
```

So let's print the shape of the training and see it's 70,000 observation has six columns now what we're going to do is from the scikit-learn dot knee plus we're going to import the caution NB which is the question a bias and we're going to put the classifier as caution NB then we'll pass on the extreme and white rain variables to the classifier and again we have the wireless co-credit which is the classifier predicts X text and we gonna compare the Y underscore predict with they underscore test to see the accuracies for that. So for that, we're going to import sq learn dot matrix we're going to import the accuracy score now let's compare both of these. So the accuracy what we get is ninety-five point five four percent now another way is to get a confusion matrix bill. So from sci-kit-learn dot matrix, we're going to import the confusion matrix and we're gonna plot the matrix of five predict and white test. So as you can see here we have 90 and 699 that's a very good number. So now what we're gonna do is create a classification report. So from metrics, we're gonna import the classification because reports we're going to put the target names as walk comma run and friends the report using white sand by predicting within target means we have. So for walking, we get the precision of 0.92 and the recall of 0.99 f1 scores is zero point nine six the support is eight thousand six hundred seventy-three and for runway appreciation of ninety percent with the recoil of 0.92 and the f1 score of zero points 95. So, guys, this is how you exactly use the Gaussian in me or the new pie's classifier on it and all of these types of algorithms which are present in the supervisor or unsurprised or reinforcement learning are all present in the cyclotron library. So one second assist SQL learn is a very important library when you are dealing with machine learning because you do not have to code any algorithm hard coding algorithm every algorithm is present there all you have to do is just passed it either split the dataset into training and testing dataset and then again you have to find the predictions . then compare the predicted Y with the test case Y. So that is exactly what we do every time we work on a machine learning algorithm now guys that were all about supervised learning let's go ahead and understand what exactly is unsupervised learning.

UNSUPERVISED LEARNING

So sometimes the given data is unstructured and unlabelled. So it becomes difficult to classify the data into different categories. So answer learning helps to solve this problem this learning is used to cluster the input data in classes on the basis of their statistical properties. So example we can cluster different bikes based upon the speed limit their acceleration or the average that they are giving.

UNSUPERVISED LEARNING: PROCESS FLOW

So I'm supporting is a type of machine learning algorithm used to draw inferences from Veda sets consisting of input data without labeled responses. So if you have a look at the workflow or the process flow of unsupervised learning.

UNSUPERVISED LEARNING PROCESS FLOW

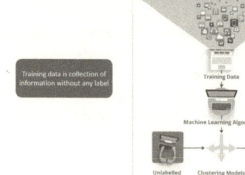

So the training data is the collection of information without any label we have the machine learning algorithm and then began the clustering models. So what it does is that distributes the data into different clusters and again if you provide any unlabeled new data it will make a prediction and find out to which cluster that particular data or the data set belongs to or the particular data point belongs to.

WHAT IS CLUSTERING?

So one of the most important algorithms in unsupervised learning is clustering. So let's understand exactly what is clustering. So a clustering basically is the process of dividing the datasets into groups consisting of similar data points it means the grouping of objects based on the information found in the data describing the objects or their relationships.

WHERE IS IT USED?

So clustering models focused on identifying groups of similar records. labeling records according to the group to which they belong now this is done without the benefit of prior knowledge about the groups and their characteristics.

WHY IS CLUSTERING USED?

So and in fact, we may not even know exactly how many groups are there to look for now these models are often referred to as unsupervised learning models since there is no external standard by which to judge the model's classification performance there are no right or wrong answers to these model. if we talk about why clustering is used.

WHERE IS IT USED?

So the goal of clustering is to determine the intrinsic group in a set of unlabelled data sometimes the partitioning is the goal or the of a clustering algorithm is to make sense of an exact value from the last set of structured. unstructured data. So that is why clustering is used in the industry and if you have a look at the various use cases of clustering in the industry. So, first of all, it's being used in marketing. So discovering distinct groups in customer databases such as customers who make a lot of long-distance calls customers who use internet more than cause they also using insurance companies for like identifying groups of cooperation insurance policyholders with high average game rate farmers crash cops which is profitable they are using cease mix studies and define probable areas of oil or gas exploration based on Seesmic data .

TYPES OF CLUSTERING

They're also used in the recommendation of movies if you would say they are also used in Flickr photos they also use by Amazon for recommending the product which category it lies in. So basically if we talk about clustering there are three types of clustering. So, first of all, we have the exclusive clustering which is the hard clustering.

TYPES OF CLUSTERING

- ● Exclusive Clustering
- ● **Overlapping Clustering**
- ● Hierarchical Clustering

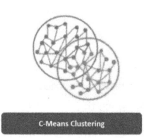

C-Means Clustering

So here an item belongs exclusively to one cluster, not several clusters and the data point belong exclusively to one cluster. So an example of this is the k-means clustering

TYPES OF CLUSTERING

● **Exclusive Clustering**

● Overlapping Clustering

● Hierarchical Clustering

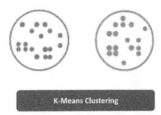

So claiming to cluster does this exclusive kind of clustering. So secondly we have overlapping clustering. So it is also known as soft clusters in this an item can belong to multiple clusters as its degree of association with each cluster is shown.

F

TYPES OF CLUSTERING

● Exclusive Clustering

● Overlapping Clustering

● **Hierarchical Clustering**

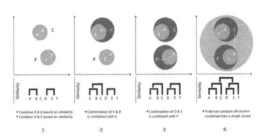

or example we have fuzzy or the C means clustering which means being used for overlapping clustering. finally, we have the hierarchical clustering. So when two clusters have a painting change relationship or a tree-like structure then it is known as a hierarchical cluster.

K-MEANS CLUSTERING

So as you can see here from the example we have a pain child kind of relationship in the cluster given here.

K-MEANS CLUSTERING

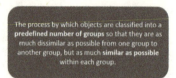

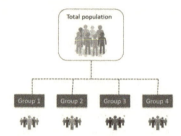

So let's understand what exactly is k-means clustering. So today means clustering is an inquiry um whose main goal is to group similar elements of data points into a cluster. it is the process by which objects are classified into a predefined number of groups.

K – MEANS ALGORITHM WORKING

So that they are as much it is similar as possible from one group to another group but as much as similar or possible within each group now if you have a look at the algorithm working here you're right.

K-MEANS ALGORITHM WORKING

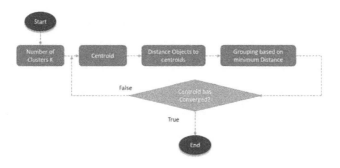

So, first of all, it starts with a defying the number of clusters which is key then again we find the centroid we find the distance objects to the distance object to the centroid distance of objects to the centroid then we find the grouping based on the minimum distance has the centroid converge if true then we make a cluster false we then I can find the centroid repeat all of the steps again and again.

K – MEANS CLUSTERING : STEPS

So let me show you how exactly clustering was with an example here. So first we need to decide the number of clusters to be made now another important task here is how to decide the important number of clusters or how to decide the number of clusters we'll get into that later.

K-MEANS CLUSTERING:STEPS

1. First we need to decide the number of clusters to be made. (Guessing)

2. Then we provide centroids of all the clusters. (Guessing)

3. The Algorithm calculates Euclidian distance of the points from each centroid and assigns the point to the closest cluster.

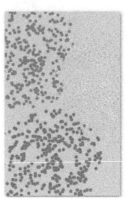

So force let's assume that the number of clusters we have decided is three. So after that then we provide the centroids for all the creditors which are guessing the algorithm calculates the Euclidean distance of the point from each centroid and assigns the data point to the closest cluster now Euclidean distance all of you know is the square root of the distance the square root of the square of the distance. So next when the centroids are calculated again we have our new clusters for each data point then again the distance from the points to the new clusters are calculated. then again the points are assigned to the closest cluster and then again we have the new centroid scatter it.

K-MEANS CLUSTERING:STEPS

1. First we need to decide the number of clusters to be made. (Guessing)

2. Then we provide centroids of all the clusters. (Guessing)

3. The Algorithm calculates Euclidian distance of the points from each centroid and assigns the point to the closest cluster.

4. Next the Centroids are calculated again, when we have our new cluster.

5. The distance of the points from the centre of clusters are calculated again and points are assigned to the closest cluster.

6. And then again the new centroid for the cluster is calculated.

7. These steps are repeated until we have a repetition in centroids or new centroids are very close to the previous ones.

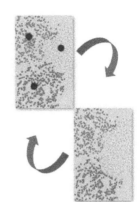

now, these steps are repeated until we have repetition in the centroids or the new centers are very close to the very previous ones. So until unless our output gets repeated or the outputs are very very close enough we do not stop this process we keep on calculating the Euclidean distance of all the points to the centroids then we calculate the new centroids.

HOW TO DECIDE THE NUMBER OF CLUSTERS

That is how claiming is clustering works basically. So an important part here is to understand how to decide the value of K or the number of clusters it does not make any sense if you do not know how many class are you going to make. So to decide the number of clusters we have the elbow method. So let's assume first of all compute the sum squared error which is the SS e for some value of K, for example, let's take two four six.

HOW TO DECIDE THE NUMBER OF CLUSTERS

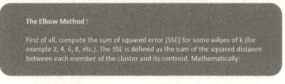

The Elbow Method :

First of all, compute the sum of squared error (SSE) for some values of k (for example 2, 4, 6, 8, etc.). The SSE is defined as the sum of the squared distance between each member of the cluster and its centroid. Mathematically:

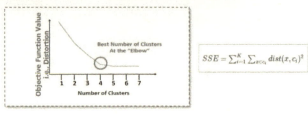

$$SSE = \sum_{i=1}^{K} \sum_{x \in c_i} dist(x, c_i)^2$$

Right now the SS e which is the sum squared error is defined as a sum of the squared distance between each number member of the cluster . its centroid mathematically. if you mathematically it is given by the equation which is provided here and if you brought the key against the SS II you will see that the error decreases as K gets large now this is because the number of cluster increases they should be smaller. So this distortion is also smaller now the idea of the elbow method is to choose the key at which the SSE decreases abruptly. So for example here if we have a look at the figure given here we see that the best number of cluster is at the elbow. So as you can see here the graph here genius abruptly after number four. So for this particular example, we're going to use for as a number of clusters. So first of all while working with k-means clustering there are two key points to know first of all be careful about where you start. So choosing the first Center at random choosing the second Center that is far away from the first Center some of it choosing the NH Center as far away from possible from the closest of the all the other centers. the second idea is to do as many runs of k-means each with different random standing points. So that you get an idea where exactly.

PROS AND CONS: K – MEANS CLUSTERING

How many clusters you need to make and where exactly the centroid lies and how the data is getting converged now he means he's not exactly a very good method. So let's understand the pros and cons of k-means clustering z' we know that k-means is simple. understandable everyone doesn't see that the first go the items automatically assigned to the clusters now if we have a look at the corns. So first of all one needs to define the number of clusters this is a very heavy task as us if we have 3/4 or if we have 10 categories and if you do not know but number of clusters are gonna be it's very difficult for anyone to you know to guess the number of clusters now all the items are forced into clusters whether they actually belong to any other cluster or any other category they are forced to lie in that other category in which they are closest to . this against happens because of the number of clusters with not defining the correct number of clusters or not being able to guess the correct number of clusters. So and most of all it's unable to handle the noisy data. the outliners because anyways and machine learning engineers and data scientists have to clean the data but then again it comes down to the analysis what they are doing . the method that they are using. So typically people do not clean the data fork-means clustering or even if the clean there are sometimes are now see noisy. outliners data which affect the whole model. So that was all for k-means clustering. So what we're gonna do is now a use k-means clustering for the movie data sets. So we have to find out the number of clusters and divide it accordingly. So the use case is that first of all we have at the air set of five thousand movies and what we want to do is group them look the movies into clusters based on the facebook lights.

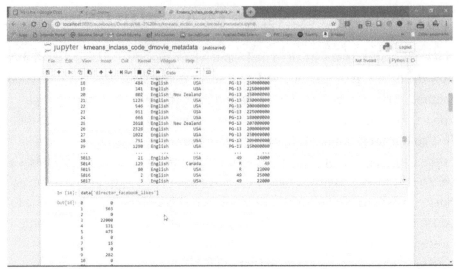

So guys let's have a look at the demo here. So first of all what we're gonna do is import deep copy numpy pandas Seabourn the various libraries which we're going to use now and from map rat levels when you use ply PI plot and we're gonna use this GD plot and next what we're gonna do is import the data set and look at the shape of the data set. So if you have a look at the shape of the data set we can see that it has five thousand and forty-three rows with 28 columns and if you have a look at the head of the data set we can see it has five thousand forty-three data points.

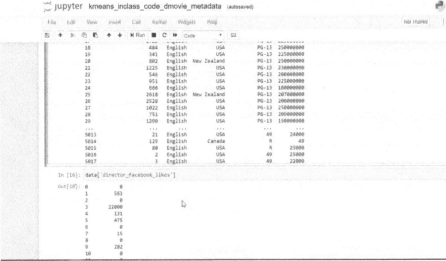

So what we're gonna do is place the data points in the plot we take the director Facebook Likes and we have a look at the data columns yeah face number in poster cast total Facebook Likes director Facebook Likes. So what we have done here now is taking the director Facebook Likes and the actor 3 Facebook Likes right. So we have five thousand forty-three rows and two columns now using the key means from s key alone what we're going to do is import it first when import key means from SQL or cluster remember guys sq done is a very important library in Python for machine learning. So and the number of clusters what we're gonna do is provide as five note this again the number of clusters depends upon the SSE which is the sum squared errors or we're going to use the elbow method. So I'm not going to go into the details of that again So we're gonna fit the data into the k-means dot fit and if you find the cluster centers then for the k-means and print it. So what we find it is an array of five clusters and if you print the label of the k-means cluster now next what we're gonna do is plot the data which we have with the clusters with the new data clusters which we have found and for this we're going to use the Seabourn and as you can see here we have plotted the card we have plotted the data into the grid and you can see here we have five clusters. So probably what I would say is that the cluster three and the cluster zero are very very close. So it might depend see that's exactly what I was going to say is that initially the main challenge and k-means clustering is to define the number of centers which are the key. So as you can see here that the third center and the zeroth. cluster the third cluster and is your cluster are very very close to each other So guys it probably could have been in one another cluster and another disadvantage was that we do not exactly know how the points are to be arranged.

FUZZY C – MEANS CLUSTERING

So it's very difficult to force the data into any other cluster which makes our analysis little different works fine but Sometimes it might be difficult to code in the k-means clustering now let's understand what exactly is siemens clustering. So the fuzzy c means is an extension of a key means clustering and the popular simple clustering technique. So fuzzy clustering also referred to as soft clustering is a form of clustering in which each data point can belong to more than one cluster.

FUZZY C - MEANS CLUSTERING

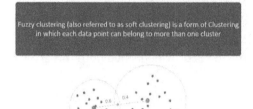

Fuzzy C-Means is an extension of K Means, the popular simple clustering technique

Fuzzy clustering (also referred to as soft clustering) is a form of Clustering in which each data point can belong to more than one cluster

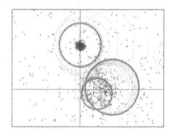

So he means tries to find the hard clusters where each point belongs to one cluster whereas the fuzzy c means to discover the soft clusters in a soft cluster any point can belong to more than one cluster at a time with a certain affinity value towards each fuzzy c means assigns the degree of membership which ranges from 0 to 1 to an object to a given cluster. So there is a stipulation that the sum of fuzzy membership of an object to all the cluster it belongs to must be equal to 1.

PROS AND CONS: C – MEANS CLUSTERING

So the degree of membership of this particular point to pool of these clusters 0.6 and 0.4 and if you add a peak at 1. So that is one of the logic behind the fuzzy c means Soon . this affinity is proportional to the distance from the point to the center of the cluster now then again we have the pros and cons of fuzzy c means. So, first of all, it allows a data point to be in multiple clusters that are a pro it's a more neutral representation of the behavior of genes usually are involved in multiple functions. So it is a very good type of clustering when we are talking about genes first of and again if we talk about the cons again we have to define C which is the number of clusters same as K next we need to determine the membership cutoff value alSo. So that takes a lot of time and it's time-consuming and the clusters are sensitive to the initial assignment of the centroid. So a slight change or deviation from the center's is going to result in a very different kind of you know a funny kind of output we get from the fuzzy.

HIERARCHICAL CLUSTERING

See means and one of the major disadvantage of a C means clustering is that it's this is a non-deterministic algorithm. So it does not give you a particular output as in such that's that now let's have a look at the third type of clustering which is the hierarchical clustering.

HIERARCHICAL CLUSTERING

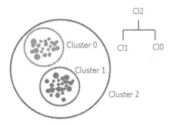

So uh hierarchical clustering is an alternative approach which builds a hierarchy from the bottom up or the top to bottom and does not require to specify the number of clusters beforehand another algorithm works as in first of all we put each data point in its own cluster. if I that closes to cluster and combine them into one more cluster repeat the above step till the data points are in a single cluster now there are two types of hierarchical clustering one is elaborated clustering and the other one is division clustering.

PROS AND CONS: HIERARCHICAL CLUSTERING

So a cumulative clustering builds the dendrogram from bottom level while the division clustering it starts all the data points in one cluster from cluster now again her archaic clustering also has some sort of pros and cons. So in the pros though no assumption of a particular number of cluster is required and it may correspond to meaningful taxonomies whereas if we talk about the course once a decision is made to combine two clusters it cannot be undone and one of the major disadvantages of these hierarchical clustering is that it becomes very slow if we talk about very very large datasets . nowadays I think every industry are using last year as it and collecting large amounts of data. So hierarchical clustering is not the app or the best method someone might need to go for. So there's that now when we talk about unsupervised learning.

MARKET BASKET ANALYSIS

So we have k-means clustering and again and there's another important term which people usually miss while talking about us was learning. there's one very important concept of market basket analysis now it is one of the key techniques used by large retailers to uncover association between items now it works by looking for combination of items that occurred together frequently in the transactions to put it it another way it allows retailers to analyze the relationships between the items that the people buy for example people who buy bread also tend to buy butter the marketing team at the retail store should target customers who buy bread and butter . provide them an offer. So that they buy a third eye like an egg. So if a customer buys bread and butter and sees a discount or an offer on eggs he will be encouraged to spend more money. buy the eggs but this is what market basket analysis is all about how to find the association between the two items and make predictions about what the customers will buy there are two algorithms which are the Association rule mining.

ASSOCIATION RULE MINING

The library algorithms. So let's discuss each of this algorithm with an example first of all if we have a look at the Association rule mining now it's a technique that shows how items are associated to each other for example customers who purchase bread have a 60% likelihood of also purchasing Jam.

ASSOCIATION RULE MINING

Association rule mining is a technique that shows how items are associated to each other.

Example:

Customer who purchase bread have a 60% likelihood of also purchasing jam.

Customer who purchase laptops are more likely to purchase laptop bags.

customers who purchase laptop are more likely to purchase laptop bags now if you take an example of an association rule if you have a look at the example here an aro B it means that if a person buys an Adam 8 then he will also buy an item P now there are three common ways o measure a particular Association because we have to find these rules on the basis of some statistics right. So what we do is use support confidence. lift now these three common ways and the measures to have a look at the Association rule mining and know exactly how good is that rule. So, first of all, we have support.

ASSOCIATION RULE MINING

Support gives fraction of transactions which contains the item A and B	*Confidence* gives how often the items A & B occur together, given no. of times A occurs	*Lift* indicates the strength of a rule over the random co-occurrence of A and B
$$Support = \frac{freq(A,B)}{N}$$	$$Confidence = \frac{freq(A,B)}{freq(A)}$$	$$Lift = \frac{Support}{Supp(A) \times Supp(B)}$$

So support gives the fraction of the transaction which contains an item a and B. So it's basically the frequency of the item in the whole item set whereas confidence gives how often the item a and B occurred together given the number of items given the number of times a occur. So it's frequency a comma B divided by the frequency of a now lift what indicates is the strength of the rule over the random co-occurrence of a and B if you have a close look at the denominator of the lift formula here we have supported an into support B now a major thing which can be noted from this is that the support of a . B are independent here. So if the value of lift or the denominator value of the lift is more it means that the items are independently selling more not together. So that in turn will decrease the value of lift. So what happens is that suppose the value of lift is more than implies that which we get it implies that the rule is strong and it can be used for later purposes because in that case.

ASSOCIATION RULE MINING EXAMPLE

The support in to support p-value which is the denominator of lift will be low which in turn means that there's a relationship between the items a and B. So let's take an example of Association rule mining and understand how exactly it works.

ASSOCIATION RULE MINING EXPALES

Set of items {A, B, C, D, E}
Set of transactions {T1, T2, T3, T4, T5}

Transactions at a local store

T1	A	B	C
T2	A	C	D
T3	B	C	D
T4	A	D	E
T5	B	C	E

So let's suppose we have a set of items a B C D and E and we have the set of transactions which are t1 t2 t3 t4 and t5 and what we need to do is create some sort of rules, for example,

ASSOCIATION RULE MINING EXAMPLE

Calculate support, confidence and lift for these rules:

Rule	Support	Confidence	Lift
A =>D	2/5	2/3	10/9
C =>A	2/5	2/4	5/6
A =>C	2/5	2/3	5/6
B, C=>A	1/5	1/3	5/9

you can see a D which means that if a person buys he buys D if a person buys C he buys.

APRIORI ALGORITHM

If it wasn't by his a he by C and for the fourth one is if a person buys a B and C he is in turn by a now what we need to do is calculate the support confidence and left of these rules now head again we talk about a priori algorithm. So a priori algorithm and the associated rule mining go hand-in-hand. So what a predator is an algorithm it uses the frequent itemsets to generate the Association rules and it is based on the concept that a subset of a frequent itemset must also be a frequent Isum set. So let's understand what is a frequent itemset. how all of these work together. So if we take the following transactions of items we have transaction T 1 T 2 T 5 and the items are 1 3 4 2 3 5 1 2 3 5 to 5 and 1 3 5.

APRIORI ALGORITHM – FIRST ITERATION

Now another more important thing about support which I forgot to mention was that when talking about Association rule mining there is a minimum support count what we need to do now the first step is to build a list of items set of size 1 using this transaction data set and use the minimum support count 2 now let's see how we do that if we create the tables see when if you have a close look at table C 1 we have the item set 1 which has a support 3 because it appears in the transaction 1 3 & 5 similarly if you have a look at the item set the single item 3. So it has a supporter of 4 it appears in 1 D 2 D 3 . T 5 but if we have a look at the items at 4 it only appears in the transaction once. So it's support value is 1 now the item set with the support rally which is less than the minimum support value that is to have to be eliminated.

APRIORI ALGORITHM – THIRD ITERATION

So the final David which is a table F 1 has 1 2 3 and 5 it does not contain the 4 now what we're going to do is create the item list of the size 2 and all the combination of the itemsets in f1 are used in this iteration. So we've left four behind we just have 1 2 3 and 5. So the possible item sets of 1 2 1 3 1 5 2 3 2 5 & 3 5 then again we'll calculate these support. So in this case, if we have a closer look at the table c2 we see that the items at 1 comma 2 are having a support value 1 which has to be eliminated.

APRIORI ALGORITHM – FIRST ITERATION

So the final table F 2 does not contain 1 comma 2 similarly if we create the itemsets of size 3 and calculate these support values but before calculating the support let's perform the piercing on the data set now what Spearing. So after all the combinations are made we divide the table see three items to check if there is another subset whose support is less than the minimum support value this is a priori algorithm. So in the item sets 1 2 3 what we can see that we have 1 2 . in the 1 to 5 again we have 1 2. So we'll discard poor of these itemsets. we'll be left with 1 3 5 & 2 3 5. So with 135 we have three subsets 1 5 1 3 3 5 which are present in table F 2 then again we have 2 3 2 5 & 3 5 which are also present in tea we'll have to. So we have to remove 1 comma 2 from table C 3.

APRIORI ALGORITHM – SECOND ITERATION

Create the table F 3 now if we're using the items of C 3 to create the adults of c4. So what we find is that we have the item set 1 2 3 5 the support value is 1 which is less than the minimum support value of 2.

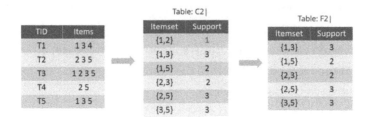

So what we're going to do is stop. we're gonna return to the previous item set that is the table c3. So the final table f3 was one three five with the support value of two . two three five with the support value of two now what waiting for a Jew is generating all the subsets of each frequent itemsets. So let's assume that our minimum confidence value is 60%. So for every subset s of Al, the output rule is that s gives I twos is that s recommends I ns if the support of I divided by the support of s is greater than or equal to the minimum confidence value then only we'll proceed further.

APRIORI ALGORITHM – THIRD ITERATION

So keep in mind that we have not used lift till now we are only working with support confidence. So applying rules with Adam sets of f3 we get rule 1 which is 1 comma 3 which gives 1 3 5 & 1 3 it means if you buy 1 & 3 there's a 66% chance that you'll buy item 5 also similarly the rule 1 comma 5 it means that if you buy 1 & 5 there's 100% chance that you will buy 3 also similarly if we have a look at rule 5 & 6 here the confidence value is less than 60% which was the assumed confidence value. So what we're going to do is we'll reject these files now an important thing to note here is that have a closer look to the rule 5 . rule 3 you see it's it has 1 5 3 1 5 3 3 1 5 it's very confusing. So one thing to keep in mind is that the order of the item sets is also very important that will help us allow create good rules and avoid any kind of confusion. So that's done So now let's learn how Association rule I used in market basket analysis problem. So what we'll do is we will be using the online transactional data of a retail store for generating Association rules. So first of all what you need to do is import pandas MLT ml X T and D libraries from the imported and read the data. So first of all what we're going to do is read the data what we're gonna do is from ml X T. e dot frequent patterns we're going to improve the a priori and Association rules as you can see here we have the head of the data you can see we have an inverse number of stock code the description quantity the inverse TTL unit price customer ID and the country. So in the next step what we will do is we will do the data cleanup which includes reviewing spaces from some of the descriptions given. what we're going to do is drop the rules that do not have the inverse numbers and remove the Freight transaction. So hey what you're gonna do is remove which do not have an invoice number if the string contains type seen was a number then we're going to remove that those are the credits remove any kind of spaces from the descriptions. So as you can see here we have like five iron. 32,000 rows with eight columns. So next what we wanted to do is after the clean up we need to consolidate the items into one transaction per row with each product for the sake of keeping the data assets small we gonna only look at the sales for France. So we're gonna use only France and group by invoice number description with the quantity sum up and C. So which leaves us with 392 rows and 1563 columns now there are a lot of zeros in the data but we also need to make sure any positive values are converted to a 1. anything less than 0 is set to 0. So for that we're going to use this code defining end code units if X is less than 0 it owns 0 if X is greater than 1 returns 1. So what we're going to do is map and apply it to the whole data set we have here. So now that we have structured the data properly. So the next step is to generate the frequent item set that has the support of at least 7% now this lumber is chosen. So that you can you get close enough now what we're gonna do is generate the ruse with the corresponding support confidence and lift. So we had given the minimum support at 0.7 the metric is lifted frequent item set and the threshold is one. So these are the following rules now a few rules with a high lift value which means that it occurs more frequently than would be expected given the number of transaction the product combinations most of the places the confidence is high as well. So these are few of the observations what we get here if we filter the data frame using the standard pandas code for large lift six and high confidence 0.8 this is what the output is going to look like these are 1 2 3 4 5 6 7 8. So as you can see here we have the eh rules which are the final rules which are given by the Association rule mining and that is how all the industries or any of these we've talked about large retailers they tend to know how their products are used . how exactly they should rearrange and provide the offers on the products. So that people spend more and more money and time in the shop. So that was all about Association rule mining. So, guys, that's all for unsupervised learning I hope you got to know about the different formulas how unsupervised learning works because you know we did not provide any label to the data all we did was create some rules . not knowing what the data is and we did clusterings different types of clusterings k-means semi's hierarchical clustering.

WHAT IS REINFORCEMENT LEARNING?

So now coming to the third and last type of learning is reinforcement learning. So what reinforcement learning is it's a type of machine learning where an agent is put in an environment. it learns to behave in this environment by performing certain actions and observing the rewards which it gets from those actions. So a reinforcement learning is all about taking appropriate action in order to maximize a reward in the particular situation . in supervised learning the training theater comprises of input and expected output. So the model is strained with the expected output itself but when it comes to reinforcement learning there is no expected output the reinforcement agent decides what actions to take in order to perform a given task in the absence of a training dataset it is bound to learn from its expertise. So let's understand reinforcement learning with an analogy.

ANALOGY

So consider a scenario wherein a baby is learning how to walk now this scenario can go in two ways first the baby starts walking in. makes it to the candy now since the candy is the end goal the baby is happy it's positive the baby is happy positive reward now coming to the second scenario the baby starts walking but falls due to some hurdle in between now the baby gets hurt and does not get to the candy it's negative the baby is sad negative reward just like we humans learn from our mistakes by a trial and an earth reinforcement learning is also similar and we have an agent which is baby a reward which is candy and many hurdles in between the agent is supposed to find the best possible path to reach the reward. So guys if you have a look at some of the important reinforcement learning definitions, first of all, we have the agent.

REINFORCEMENT LEARNING DEFINITIONS

So the reinforcement learning algorithm that learns from trial in that's the agent now if we talk about environment the world through which the agent moves or the obstacles

REINFORCEMENT LEARING DEFINITIONS

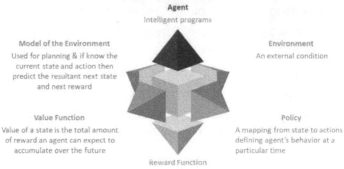

Agent
Intelligent programs

Model of the Environment
Used for planning & if know the current state and action then predict the resultant next state and next reward

Environment
An external condition

Value Function
Value of a state is the total amount of reward an agent can expect to accumulate over the future

Policy
A mapping from state to actions defining agent's behavior at a particular time

Reward Function
Could be +1 or any other value, indicating, what's good in an immediate sense

which the agent has to conquer or the environment now actions a are all the possible steps that the agent can take the state s is the current conditions returned by the environment then again we have reward R and instant return for the environment to appraise the last action then again we have policy which is PI it is the approach that the agent uses to remind the next action based on the current state we have value V which is the expected long-term

REINFORCEMENT LEARNING DINITIONS

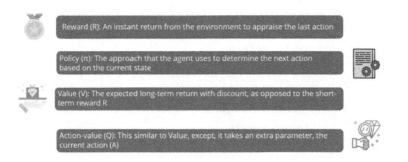

Reward (R): An instant return from the environment to appraise the last action

Policy (π): The approach that the agent uses to determine the next action based on the current state

Value (V): The expected long-term return with discount, as opposed to the short-term reward R

Action-value (Q): This similar to Value, except, it takes an extra parameter, the current action (A)

return with discount as open to the short-term what are then again we have the action value Q this is similar to value except it takes an extra parameter which is the current state action which is a now let's talk about reward maximization for a moment.

REWARD MAXIMIZATION

Now reinforcement learning agent works based on the theory of reward maximization this is exactly why the RL must be trained in such a way that he takes the best action. So that the reward is maximum now the collective rewards at a particular time and the respective action is written as G T equals RT plus one RT plus two and. Soon now the equation is an ideal representation of rewards generally things do not work out like this while summing up the cumulative rewards now let me explain this with a small gape in the figure you see a fox right Some meat and a Tyler our reinforcement learning agent is the Fox and his end goal is to eat the massive Otto meat before being eaten by the tiger since this fox is clever fellow he eats the meat that is closer to him rather than the meat which is close to the tiger because the closer he goes to the Tiger the higher are his chances of getting killed as a result of the reward near the tiger in if they are bigger meat chunks will be discounted this is done because of the uncertainty factor that the tiger might kill the Fox

EXPLORATION AND EXPLOITATION

Now the next thing to understand is how discounting of reward works now to do this we define a discount called the gamma the value of gamma is

THE EPSILON GREEDY ALGORITHM

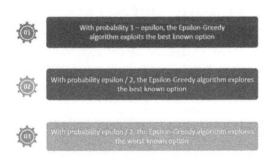

With probability 1 – epsilon, the Epsilon-Greedy algorithm exploits the best known option

With probability epsilon / 2, the Epsilon-Greedy algorithm explores the best known option

With probability epsilon / 2, the Epsilon-Greedy algorithm explores the worst known option

between 0 & 1 the smaller the gamma the larger the discount and vice versa.

THE EPSILON GREEDY ALGORITHM

01 Tries to be fair to the two opposite goals of exploration and exploitation by using a mechanism of flipping a coin

02 Just like, if you flip a coin and it comes up head you should explore for a moment but if it comes up tails, you should exploit

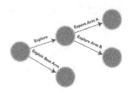

Takes whatever action seems best at the present moment

So our cumulative discounted reward is GT summation of K 0 to infinity gamma to the power P as DK t plus k plus 1 where gamma belongs to 0 to 1 but if the Fox decides to explore a bit it can find bigger rewards that is this big chunk of meats this is called exploration. So the reinforcement learning basically works on the basis of exploration and exploitation. So exploitation is about using the already known expert information to heighten the rewards whereas exploration is all about exploring and capturing more information about the environment there is another problem which is known as the K armed bandit problem the K armed bandit it is a metaphor representing a casino slot machine with K pull levers or arms the users or the customer pulls

THE K- ARMED BANDIT PROBLEM

Any one of the levers to win a projected reward the objective is to select the leeward that will provide the user with the highest reward now here comes the epsilon-greedy algorithm it tries to be fair to do opposite cause of exploration-exploitation by using a mechanism of flipping a coin which is like if you flip a coin.

THE EPSILON GREEDY ALGORITHM

Comes up head you should explore for memory butter comes up days you should exploit it takes whatever action seems best at the present moment. So with probability while epsilon the epsilon-greedy algorithm exploits the best-known option with probability epsilon by 2 epsilon 0 it explores the best known option . with the probability epsilon by 2 with probability epsilon by 2 the algorithm explores the best-known option and with the probability epsilon by 2 the epsilon-greedy algorithm explores the worst known option now let's talk about Markov decision process the mathematical approach for mapping a solution in reinforcement learning is called Markov decision process which is MDP in a way the purpose of reinforcement learning is to Solve a Markov decision process now the following parameters are used to attain a solution set of actions a set of states

MARKOV DECISION PROCESS

MARKOV DECISION PROCESS

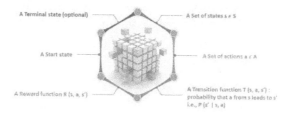

The mathematical approach for mapping a solution in reinforcement learning is called *Markov Decision Process* (MDP)

The following parameters are used to attain a solution:

We have the reward our policy PI . the value V and we have translational function T probability that our forum leads to snow to briefly sum it up the agent must take up an action to transition from the start state to end state s while doing. So the agent receives the reward R for each action he takes the series of actions taken by the agent to define the policy PI.

MARKOV DECISION PROCESS – SHORTEST PATH PROBLEM

The rewards collected by collected to find the value of V the main goal here is to maximize the rewards by choosing the optimum policy now let's take an example of choosing the shortest path now consider the given example here. So what we have is given the above representation our goal here is to find the shortest path between a. D each edge has a number linked to it and this

MARKOV DECISION PROCESS
SHORTEST PATH PROBLEM

Goal: Find the shortest path between A and D with minimum possible cost

In this problem,

- Set of states are denoted by nodes i.e. {A, B, C, D}

- Action is to traverse from one node to another {A -> B, C -> D}

- Reward is the cost represented by each edge

- Policy is the path taken to reach the destination {A -> C -> D}

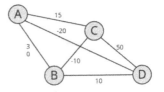

denotes the cost to traverse that edge now the task at hand is to traverse from point A to D with the minimum possible cost in this problem the set of states are denoted by the nodes ABCD ad the action is to traverse from one node to another are given by an arrow B or C our OD reward is the cost represented by each edge . the policy is the path taken to reach each destination a to C to D. So you start off at node a and take baby steps to your destination initially only the next possible node is visible to you if you follow the greedy approach. take the most optimal step that is choosing a to see instead of a to B or C now you are at node C and want to traverse to node T you must again choose the path wisely choose the path with the lowest cost we can see that a CD has the lowest cost. hence we take that path to conclude the policy is a to C to D. the value is 120.

UNDERSTANDING Q- LEARNING WITH AN EXAMPLE

So let's understand Q learning algorithm which is one of the most use reinforcement learning algorithm with the help of examples. So we have five rooms in a building connected by toast . each room is numbered from 0

UNDERSTANDING Q-LEARNING

WITH AN EXAMPLE

Add another matrix Q, representing the memory of what the agent has learned through experience.
- The rows of matrix Q represent the current state of the agent
- columns represent the possible actions leading to the next state
- Formula to calculate the Q matrix:

Q(state, action) = R(state, action) + Gamma * Max [Q(next state, all actions)]

through 4 the outside of the building can be thought of as one big room which is tea room number five now dose 1 & 4 lead into the building from the room 5 outside now let's represent the rooms on a graph . each node each room has a node and each door as link. So as you can see here we have represented it as a graph. our goal is to reach the node 5 which is the outer space. So what we're gonna do is and the next step is to associate a reward value to each toe. So the dose that directed read to you will have a reward of 100 whereas the doors that do not directly connect to the target have a reward and because the dose had to weigh two arrows are assigned to each room.

UNDERSTANDING Q-LEARNING
WITH AN EXAMPLE

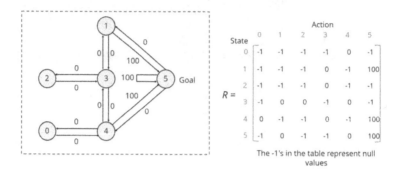

State	Action					
	0	1	2	3	4	5
0	-1	-1	-1	-1	0	-1
1	-1	-1	-1	0	-1	100
$R =$ 2	-1	-1	-1	0	-1	-1
3	-1	0	0	-1	0	-1
4	0	-1	-1	0	-1	100
5	-1	0	-1	-1	0	100

The -1's in the table represent null values

each row contains an instant about the valley. So after that, the terminology in the q-learning includes the term states and action. So room 5 represents a state agents movement from one room to another room represents in action and in this figure a state is depicted as a node while the action is represented by the arrows.

UNDERSTANDING Q-LEARNING
WITH AN EXAMPLE

The terminology in Q-Learning includes the terms state and action:
- Room (including room 5) represents a state
- agent's movement from one room to another represents an action
- In the figure, a state is depicted as a node, while "action" is represented by the arrows

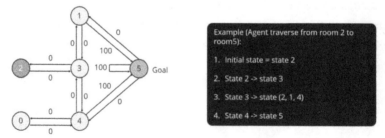

Example (Agent traverse from room 2 to room5):

1. Initial state = state 2
2. State 2 -> state 3
3. State 3 -> state (2, 1, 4)
4. State 4 -> state 5

So, for example, let's say can eat in that Traverse from room to the roof. I So the initial state is gonna be the state to it then the next step is from stage 2 to stage 3 next is to moves from stage 3 to stage either 2 1 or 4. So if it goes to the 4 it reaches stage 5 So that's how you represent the hole traversing of any particular agent in all of these rooms a represents their actions via notes. So we can put this state diagram. instant reward values into a reward table which is the matrix R. So as you can see the minus 1 here in the table represents the null values because you cannot go from 1 to 1 right and since there is no way from to go from 1 to 0.

UNDERSTANDING Q-LEARNING WITH AN EXAMPLE

Next step is to associate a reward value to each door:

- doors that lead directly to the goal have a reward of 100

- Doors not directly connected to the target room have zero reward

- Because doors are two-way, two arrows are assigned to each room

- Each arrow contains an instant reward value

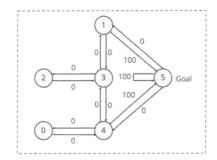

So that is also minus 1 so minus 1 represents the null values whereas the 0 represents zero rewards and 100 represents the reward going to the room five. So one more important thing to know here is that if you've enrolled fireman you could go to room five the reward is hundred. So what we need to do is add another matrix Q representing the memory of what the agent has learned to experience the rows of matrix Q represent the current state of the agent whereas the columns represent the possible action leading to the next state now if the formula to calculate the Q matrix is if a particular Q at a particular state . the given action is equal to the R of that state in action plus gamma which we discussed earlier the Kurama parameter which we discussed earlier which ranges from 0 to 1 into the maximum of the Q or the next state comma all actions. So let's understand this with an example so here are the nine steps which any Q learning algorithm particularly has.

Q – LEARNING EXAMPLE

So, first of all, is to set the gamma parameter. the environment rewards in the matrix R then we need to do is initialize the matrix Q to 0 select the random initial state set the initial state to current state select one among all the possible actions for the current state using this possible action consider going to the next state when you get the next state get the maximum Q value for this next state based upon all the actions compute the Q value using the formula repeat the above steps until the current state equals your code.

Q- LEARNING ALGORITHM

1. Set the gamma parameter, and environment rewards in matrix R
2. Initialize matrix Q to zero
3. Select a random initial state
4. Set initial state = current state
5. Select one among all possible actions for the current state
6. Using this possible action, consider going to the next state
7. Get maximum Q value for this next state based on all possible actions
8. Compute: Q(state, action) = R(state, action) + Gamma * Max[Q(next state, all actions)]
9. Repeat above steps until current state = goal state

So the first step is to set the values of the learning parameters gamma which is 0.8. the initial state as room number one. So the next initialize the Q matrix a zero matrix. So on the left hand side as you can see here we have the Q matrix which has all the values as 0 now from room 1 you can either go to room 3 or room 5. So let's select room 5 because that's our end goal so from room 5 calculate the maximum cube value for this next state based on all possible actions.

Q- LEARNING EXAMPLE

For the next episode, the next state, 1, now becomes the current state. We repeat the inner loop of the Q
learning algorithm because state 1 is not the goal state.
• From room 1 you can either go to room 3 or 5, let's select room 5.
• From room 5, calculate maximum Q value for this next state based on all possible actions:
Q(state, action) = R(state, action) + Gamma * Max[Q(next state, all actions)]

Q(1,5) = R(1,5) + 0.8 * Max[Q(5,1), Q(5,4), Q(5,5)] = 100 + 0.8 * 0 = 100
The matrix Q remains the same since, Q(1,5) is already fed to the agent

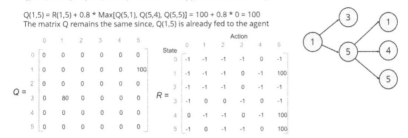

$$Q = \begin{bmatrix} & 0 & 1 & 2 & 3 & 4 & 5 \\ 0 & 0 & 0 & 0 & 0 & 0 & 0 \\ 1 & 0 & 0 & 0 & 0 & 0 & 100 \\ 2 & 0 & 0 & 0 & 0 & 0 & 0 \\ 3 & 0 & 80 & 0 & 0 & 0 & 0 \\ 4 & 0 & 0 & 0 & 0 & 0 & 0 \\ 5 & 0 & 0 & 0 & 0 & 0 & 0 \end{bmatrix}$$

$$R = \begin{bmatrix} & 0 & 1 & 2 & 3 & 4 & 5 \\ 0 & -1 & -1 & -1 & -1 & 0 & -1 \\ 1 & -1 & -1 & -1 & 0 & -1 & 100 \\ 2 & -1 & -1 & -1 & 0 & -1 & -1 \\ 3 & -1 & 0 & 0 & -1 & 0 & -1 \\ 4 & 0 & -1 & -1 & 0 & -1 & 100 \\ 5 & -1 & 0 & -1 & -1 & 0 & 100 \end{bmatrix}$$
(State / Action)

So Q 1 comma 5 equals R 1 comma 5 which is hundred plus zero point eight which is the gamma into the maximum of Q 5 comma 1 5 commas 4 and 5 commas 5. So maximum or five commas one five commas four five commas five is hundred. So the Q values from initially as you can see here the Q values are initialized to zero. So it does not matter as of now so the maximum is zero. So the final Q value for Q 1 comma 5 is 100 that's how we're gonna update our Q matrix so Q matrix the position has 1 comma 5 in the second row gets updated to 100. So the first step we have turned right now that for the next episode we start with a randomly chosen initial state so let's assume that the stage is 3. So from rule number 3 you can either go to room number 1 2 or 4. So let's select the option of room number 1 because from our previous experience what we've seen is that one has directly connected to room 5. So from room / 1 calculate the maximum Q value for this next state based on all possible action. So 3 commas 1 if we take we get our 3 4 1 plus 0 points 8 commas into a maximum of T's we get the value as 80. So the matrix Q gets updated now for the next episode the next state 1 now becomes the current state we repeat the inner loop of the Q learning algorithm because tip 1 is not the goal state from 1 you can either go to 3 of 5. So let's select 105 as that's our goal so from room row 5 again we can go from all of these. So the Q matrix remains the same since Q 1 5 is already fed to the agent. that is how you select the random starting points and fill up the Q Q matrix and see where which path will lead us there with the maximum provide points now what we gonna do is do the same coding using the Python in machine learning. So what we're going to do is prove an umpire's NP we're gonna take

the R matrix as we defined earlier. So that the minus 1 is the nerve values zeros are the values which provide a 0 and hundreds are the value. So what we're going to do is initialize the Q matrix now to 0 we're going to put gamma as 0.8. set the initial state as 1 now here returns all the available

actions in the state given as an argument. So if we define the of action with the given state we get the available action in the current state. So we have another function here which is known as a sample next action what this function does is that chooses at random which action to be performed within the range of all the available actions and finally we have action which is the sample next action with the available act now again we have another function which is updated now what it does is that it updates the Q matrix according to the path selected . a Q learning algorithm. So initially our Q matrix is all 0 so what we're gonna do is we're gonna train it over 10,000 iterations and let's see what exactly gives the output of the Q value. So if then the agent learns more through for the iterations it will finally breach converges value in Q matrix. So the Q matrix can then be normalized at is converted to a percentage by dividing all the non-zeros entities by the highest number which is 500 in this case. So once the matrix Q gets close enough to the state of convergence agent has learned the most optimal path to the goal State. So what we're gonna do next is divide it by 5 which is the maximum here so Q R . P Q max in 200. So that we get a normalized now once the Q matrix gets close enough to the state of convergence the agent has learned or the paths. So the optimal path is given by the Q learning employer Thomas if it starts from 2 it will go to 3 then go to 1. then goes to 5 if it starts at 2 it can go to 3 then 4 then 5 that will give us the same results. so as you can see here is the output given by the Q learning algorithm is the selected path is 2 3 1. Feinstein from the Q State - So this is how exactly a reinforcement learning algorithm works it finds the optimal solution using the path. given the action and rewards and the various other definitions or the various other challenges I would say actually the main goal is to get the master reward. get the maximum value through the environment and that's how an agent learns through its own path and going millions. millions of iterations learning how each part will give us what reward. So that's how the Q learning algorithm works. that's how it works in Python as well as I showed you. So now that you have a clear idea of the different machine learning algorithms how it works the different phases of machine learning the different applications of machine learning how supervised learning works how unsupervised learning works our reinforcement learning works. what to choose in what scenario what are the different algorithms under all of these

AI AND ML AND DL

Types of machine learning next move forward to the next part our session Rich's understanding about artificial intelligence deep learning and machine learning well data science is Something that has been there for ages nonetheless.

AI AND ML AND DL

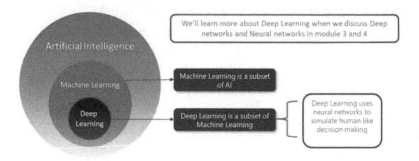

data science is the extraction of knowledge from data by using scientific techniques and algorithms people usually have a certain level of dilemma or I would say a certain level of confusion when it comes to differentiating between the terms artificial intelligence machine learning. deep learning. So don't worry I'll clear all of these doubts for you artificial intelligence is a technique which enables machine to mimic human behavior now the idea behind artificial intelligence is fairly simple yet fascinating which is to make intelligent machines that can take decisions on their own now for years it was thought that computers would never match the power of the human brain well back then we did not have enough data . computational power but now with big data coming into existence and with the advent of GPUs artificial intelligence is possible now machine learning is a subset of artificial intelligence technique which uses statistical method to enable machines to improve with experience whereas deep learning is a subset of machine learning which makes the computation of multi-layer neural network feasible it uses the neural networks to stimulate human-like decision-making. So as you can see if we talk about the data science ecosystem we have artificial intelligence machine learning. deep learning being the innermost circle is very much required for machine learning as well as artificial in but why was deep learning required. So for that less understand the need for a deep lolly. So a step towards artificial intelligence was machine learning and machine learning was a subset of a play it deals with the extraction of patterns from the last dataset Haslam la dataset was not a problem what was a problem was machine learning algorithms could not handle the high dimensional data where we have a large number of inputs. outputs which round thousands of dimensions handling and processing such

LIMITATIONS OF MACHIN LEARNING

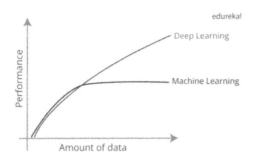

type of data becomes very complex and resource exhaustion now this is also termed as the curse of dimensionality now another challenge faced by machine learning was to specify the features to be extracted.

So as we saw earlier in all the algorithms which are discussed now we had to specify the features to be extracted now this plays an important role in protecting the outcome as well as in achieving better actress therefore without feature extraction the challenge for the program increases as the effectiveness of the algorithm very much depends on how insightful the program is now this is where deep learning comes into picture.

WHAT IS DEEP LEARNING?

DEEP LEARNING TO RESCUE

- Deep Learning is one of the only methods by which we can circumvent the challenges of feature extraction.
- This is because Deep Learning models are capable of learning to focus on the right features by themselves, requiring little guidance from the programmer.

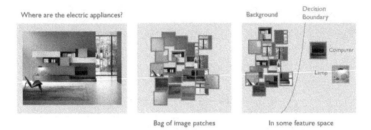

Comes to the rescue but deep learning is capable of handling the high dimensional data and is also efficient in focusing on the right features on its own. So what exactly is deeper so deep learning is a subset of machine

WHAT IS DEEP LEARNING

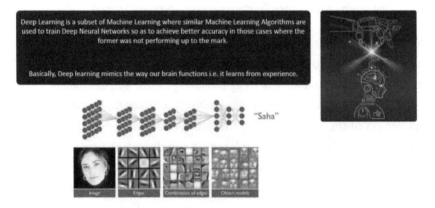

learning as I mentioned earlier where similar machine learning algorithms are used to Train deep neural networks. So as to achieve better accuracy in those cases where the former was not performing up to the MA basically deep learning mimics the way our brain functions. learns from experience. So as you know our brain is made up of billions of neurons that allows us to do amazing things when the brain of a small kid is capable of solving complex problems which are very difficult to solve even using the supercomputers. So how can we achieve the same functionality in programs now this is where we understand artificial neuron and artificial neural networks.

APPLICATIONS OF DEEP LEARNING

So, first of all, let's have a look at the different applications of deep learning we have automatic machine translation object classification before automatic handwriting generation character text generation we have image caption generation colorization of black. white images we have an automatic

APPLICATIONS OF DEEP LEARNING

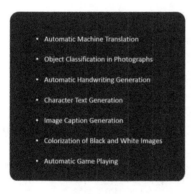
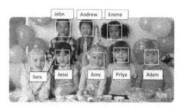

game playing and much more now google lens is a set of vision based computing capabilities that allows your smartphone to understand what's going on in a photo video or any live feed, for instance, point your phone at a flower. google lens will tell you on the screen which type of flower it is you can in that camera at any restaurant sign to see the reviews and other recommendations now if we talk word mushroom transition this is a task where you are given words in some language. you have to translate the words to the desired language see English but this kind of translation is a classic example of image recognition and final application of deep learning which we have here is image polarization. So automatic colorization of black.

white images as you know earlier we did not have color photographs back there in The 40s and 50s we did not have any color photographs. So through deep learning analyzing water shadows is present in the image how the light is bouncing off the skin tone of the people automatic colorization is now possible.

HOW NEURON WORKS?

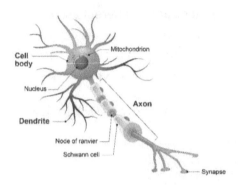

this is all possible because of deep learning now deep learning studies the basic unit of a brain cell called a neuron now let us understand the functionality of a biological neuron. how we mimic this functionality in the perception or what we call is an artificial neuron. So as you can see here we have the image of a biological neuron. So it has a cell body it has mitochondrion nucleus we have dendrites there we have the axon we have the node of the ran of the ear you have the scavenge cell. the synapse. So we need not know about all of these. So what we need to know most about is dendrite which receives signals from other neurons we have a cell body which sums up all the inputs. we have axon which is used to transmit the signals to the other cells now an artificial neuron or perceptron is a linear model which is based upon the same principle . is used for binary classification it models a neuron which has a set of inputs each of which is given a specific weight.

A PERCEPTRON

the neuron computes Some functions on these weighted inputs. gives the outputs it receives n inputs corresponding to each feature it then sums up those inputs applies the transformation.

A PERCEPTRON

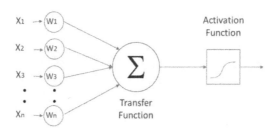

Schematic for a neuron in a neural net

produces an output it has generally two functions which are the summation. the transformation but the transformation is also known as activation functions. So as you can see here we have certain inputs we have certain weights we have the transfer function. then we have the activation function now the transfer function is nothing but the summation function here. it is the schematic for a neuron in a neural network.

ROLE OF WEIGHTS AND BIAS

So this is how we mimic a biological neuron in terms of programming now the way it shows the effectiveness of a particular input move the weight of

ROLE OF WEIGHTS AND BIAS

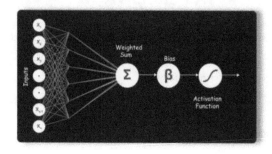

input more it will have an impact on the neural network on the other hand bias is an additional parameter in the perception which is sed to address the output along with the weighted sum of the inputs to the neuron which helps the model in a way that it can best fit for the given data activation functions translate the inputs into outputs and it uses a threshold to produce an output there are many functions that use has activation functions such as linear or identity we have unit or binary step we have sigmoid logistic tan edge ray Lu . soft Max now if we talk about the linear transformation or the activation function.

ACTIVATION FUNCTIONS

- Activation function translates the inputs into outputs
- It uses a threshold to produce an output

1. Linear or Identity
2. Unit or Binary Step
3. Sigmoid or Logistic
4. Tanh
5. ReLU
6. SoftMax

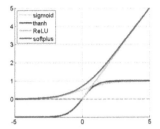

So a linear transform is basically the identity function where the dependent variable has a directly proportional relationship with the independent variable now in practical terms it means that a function passes the signal through unchanged now the question arises when to use linear transform function simple answer is when we want to solve a linear regression problem we apply a linear transformation function . next in our list of activated functions we have your next step the output of a unit step function is either 1 or 0 now it depends on the threshold value we define a step function with the threshold value five is shown here. So let's consider X is five. So if the value is less than five the output will be zero whereas if the value is equal to or greater than five then the valuable one this equal to is very much important to consider here because sometimes people put up the equal two in the lower end of the side. So that's not it how it is used but rather it's used on the upper hand side where if the value is greater than particular X greater than or equal to X then only the value will be one now a sigmoid function is a machine that converts an independent variable of near infinite range into simple probabilities between 0 & 1 now most of its output will be very close to either 0 or 1 . if you have a look at the function here we have 1 divided by n plus y raise to power minus beta X. So I'm not going to the details or the mathematical function of a particular sigmoid but it's very much used to convert the independent variables of very large infinite range to the values between 0 & 1 now the question arises when to use a sigmoid transformation function. So when we want to map the input values to a value in the range of 0 to 1 where we know the output should lie only between these two numbers we apply the sigmoid transformation function note an H is a hyperbolic trigonometric function now unlike the sigmoid function the

ACTIVATION FUNCTIONS

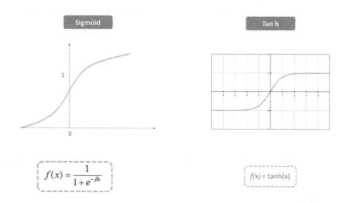

normalized range of tan H is minus 1 to 1 it's very much similar to the sigmoid function but the advantage of tan H is that it can deal more easily with negative numbers now next on our list we have Ray Lu now rail you or the rectify linear unit transform function only activates our node if the input is above a certain quantity while the input is below 0 the output is 0 but when the input Rises about a certain threshold or if we take In this case at 0 but if you have a certain value X if it crosses that certain threshold it has a linear relationship with the dependent variable now this is very much different from a normal linear transformation. So has a certain threshold now the question arises here again when to use a railroad transformation function.

ACTIVATION FUNCTIONS

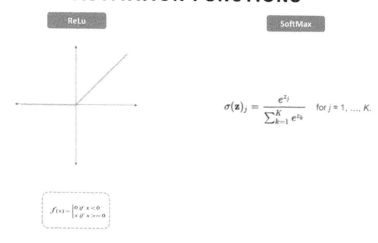

So when we want to map the input values to a value in the range So as input X to maximum 0 comma X that is it Maps the negative inputs to 0 and the positive inputs are output without any change we apply a rectified linear unit or the railroad transformation function now the final one which we have is sort max. So when we have four or five classes of outputs the softmax function will give the probability distribution of each it is useful for finding out the class which has the maximum probability. So soft mass is a function you will often find at the output layer of a classifier now suppose we have an input of say the letters of English words. we want to classify which letter it is. So for that case we're going to use the sort max function because in the output we have certain classes but I would say in English if we take English we had 26 classes from A to Z.

PERCEPTRON EAMPLE

So in that case softmax activation function is very much important now artificial neuron can be used to implement logic gates now I'm sure you guys

PERCEPTRON

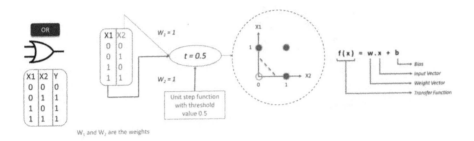

must be familiar with the working of all K that is the output is one if any of the input is also one, therefore, a perception can be used as a separator or a decision line that divides the input set of or gate into two classes the first class being the inputs having output as 0 that lies below the division line . the second class would input having output as 1 that lies above the decision line or the separator. So mathematically a perceptron can be thought of like an equation of weights inputs. bias as you can see here we have f of X is equal to weight into the input vector plus the bias. So let's go ahead with our demo understand how we can implement this perceptron example which is of an or gate using neural networks using artificial neuron or the perception. here we're going to use tensor flow along with Python.

WHAT ARE TENSORS?

So let's understand what exactly is tensor flow first before going it to the demo. So basically tensor flow is a deep learning framework by Google to understand it in a very easy way let's understand the two terms of sensor

WHAT ARE TENSORS?

Tensors are the standard way of representing data in deep learning

Tensors are just multidimensional arrays, an extension of 2-dimensional tables (matrices) to data with higher dimension.

't'
'e'
'n'
's'
'o'
'r'

Tensor Of Dimension -6

Tensor Of Dimension –[6,4]

Tensor Of Dimension –[6,4,2]

flow which are the tensors. the flow. So starting with tensors are a standard way of representing theatre in deep learning and they are just multi-dimensional arrays it is an extension of two-dimensional table matrices through the data with a higher dimension. So as you can see have first of all we have a tensor of dimension 6 then we have a tensor of dimension 6 commas 4 which is 2d. again we have a tensor of dimension 6 4 and 2 which is reading now this dimension is not restricted to 3 we can have four dimensions five dimensions it depends upon the number of inputs or the number of classes or the parameters which we provide to a particular neural net or a particular perception. So which brings us sensor flow intensive flow the computation is approached as a data flow graph. So we have a tensor. then again we have a flow in which we suppose for taking the example here we have the data we do addition then we do matrix multiplication then we check the result if it's good then it's fine. if the result is not good then we again do some sort of matrix multiplication or addition it depends upon the function that we are using and then finally we have the output.

WHAT ARE TENSOR FLOW?

So if you want to know about it as a flow we have an entire playlist on tensor flow. deep-learning which you should see I'll give the link to all of these videos in the description box. So let's go ahead with our demo. understand how we can implement the or gates using perception. So first of all what we're going to do is import all the required libraries and Here I am going to

WHAT IS TENSORFLOW?

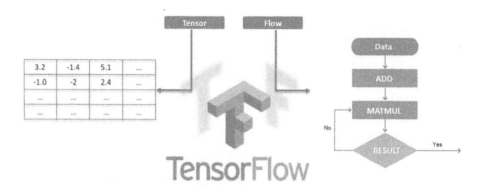

import only one library which is the tensor flow library. So what we're going to do is import sensor flow a steal now the next step that we're going to do is define vector variables for Input and output. So for that, we need to create variables for storing the input-output. the bias for the perception. So as you can see here we have the training input and again we have the training

```
In [2]: import tensorflow as tf

In [14]: train_in = [
             [0,0,1],
             [0,1,1],
             [1,0,1],
             [1,1,1]]

In [15]: train_out = [
             [0],
             [1],
             [1],
             [1]]

In [22]: w = tf.Variable(tf.random_normal([3, 1], seed=15))

In [23]: x = tf.placeholder(tf.float32,[None,3])
         y = tf.placeholder(tf.float32,[None,1])

In [24]: output = tf.nn.relu(tf.matmul(x, w))

In [25]: loss = tf.reduce_sum(tf.square(output - y))

In [26]: optimizer = tf.train.GradientDescentOptimizer(0.01)
         train = optimizer.minimize(loss)

In [27]: init = tf.global_variables_initializer()
```

output now what we're going to do next is define the weight variable and here we are we will define the tensor variable of the shape 3 commas 1 . for our weights and we will assign some random values to it initially. So we're going to use the T AF dot variable. we're going to use TF run random normal to assign random variables to the 3 cross 1 tensor next what we do is define placeholders for input and output and. So that they can accept external inputs on the run so this will be T F dot float32. So for X, we are going to use a dimension for 3 and for y it's the dimension of 1 now as discussed earlier the input received by a positron is force multiplied by the respective weights. then all of these weights input our sum together now this sum value is then fed to the activation for obtaining the final result of the or gate perceptron. So this is the output here what we are defining. So it's TF dot neural networks dot rely upon using the rely upon activation function here. we are doing the matrix multiplication of the weights. biases, in this case, I have used the Rayleigh function but you are free to use any of the activation functions according to your needs the next what we're going to do is calculate the cost or ere. So we need to calculate the cost which is the mean squared error which is nothing but the square of the differences or the perceptron output. the desired output. So the equation will be loss equals DF dot reduce some. we'll use the TF dot Square output minus now the cool of a perceptron is to minimize the loss or the cost or the error. So here we are going to use the gradient descent optimizer which will reduce the loss. it is a very important part of any neural network to use any sort of optimizer. So here we are using the gradient descent optimizer you can know more about the gradient descent optimizer in other a Drake of videos or deep learning. neural networks now the next step comes is to initialize the variables. so variables are only defined with TF dot variables the initially what weighted. So we need to initialize this variable define. So for that, we're going to use the T F dot global variable initializer. we're going to create the F dot session and we will not run with the initialization variables. So as all the variables are initialized not coming to the last step what we're going to do is we need to train our perception that is an update away our values of the weights and the biases in the successive iteration to minimize the error or the Ross. So here I will be training our perceptron in hundred epochs. So as you can see here for I in range hundred we are going to run the session with training data in. why as a trainee at the output and we're going to calculate the loss and feed it directly to the X train and why train and again and print the epoch. So as you can see here for the first iteration the loss was two points zero seven and coming down if as soon as the iterations increase the loss is decreasing because of the gradient optimizer it's learning how the data is. coming down to the hundredths or the final epoch here we have the loss of zero point two seven starts with two-point zero seven here initially and we ended up with zero points two seven loss which is very good this was how perceptron works on a particularly given data set it learns about it . as you saw earlier we have a set of input the Input variables we provided weights we had a summation function and then we use the rail u activation function in the code to get the final output and then we trained the particular model for hundred iterations with the training data.

PERCPTRON PROBLEMS

So as to minimize the loss and the loss came down all the way from two-point seven to zero point two seven well if you think perceptron Solves all the problem of making a human brain then you were wrong there are two

PERCEPTRON PROBLEMS

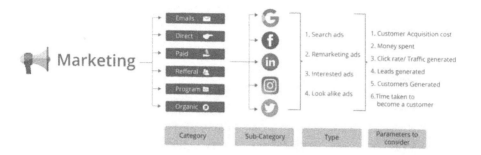

major problems first problem is that the single-layer perceptron cannot classify non linearly separable data points. which other complex problems that involve a lot of parameters cannot be Solved by a single layer perceptron now consider the example here and the complexity with the parameters involved to take a decision by the marketing team. So as you can see here for every email direct paid referral program or organic we have a certain number of social media subcategories Google Facebook LinkedIn we have twitter. then we have the type such as the search and remarketing as interest as ad look like ads and again the parameters to be considered are the customer acquisition cost money span leads generated customers generated time taken to become a customer and all of these problems cannot be solved by a single layer of perceptron our one neuron cannot take in. So many inputs. that is why more than one neuron would be used to solve this kind of problem.

DEEP NEURAL NETWORK

So the neural network is really just a composition of perceptron connected in different ways and operating on activation functions. So for that, we have three different terminologies in a particular neural network we have the

DEEP NEURAL NETOWRK

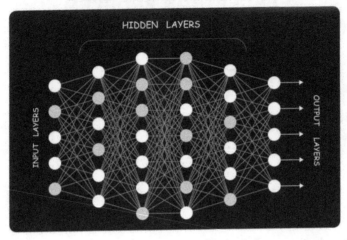

input layers we have the hidden layers. we have the output layers. So in a hidden layer, we have hidden nodes that provide information from the outside world to the network. heart together referred to as the input layer now the hidden nodes perform computations. transfer information from the input nodes to the output nodes now a collection of hidden nodes forms an idle layer in our image we have one two three four hidden layers. finally, the output nodes are collectively referred to as output layers. They are responsible for computation and transferring information from the network to the outside world now that you have an idea of how a perceptron behaves the different parameters involved. the different layers of neural networks let's continue this session and see how we can create our own neural network from scratch in this image as you can see here we have given a list of faces first of all the patterns of local contrast is being computed in the input layer then in the hidden layer 1 we get the face features . in the hidden layer 2 we get the different features of the face and finally we have the output layer now if we talk about training networks.

TRAINING NETWORK WEIGHTS

Weights in particular neural networks we can estimate the weight values for our training data using stochastic gradient descent optimizer as I mentioned earlier now it requires two parameters which are the learning rate. as I

TRAINING NETWORK WEIGHTS

- We can estimate the weight values for our training data using 'stochastic gradient descent' optimizer.

- Stochastic gradient descent requires two parameters:

- **Learning Rate**: Used to limit the amount each weight is corrected each time it is updated.

- **Epochs**: The number of times to run through the training data while updating the weight.

- These, along with the training data will be the arguments to the function.

mentioned earlier learning rate is used to limit the amount of each weight is corrected each time it is updated. epoch is several times to run through the training data while updating the way. So in the previous example, we had 100 boxes so we trained the whole model a hundred times. these along with the training data will be the arguments to the function as data scientists or data analysts or machine learning engineers working on the hyper parameters is the most important part because anyone can do the coding it's your experience. your way of thinking about the learning rate. the epochs the model which you are working the input data you are taking how much time it will require to train because time is limited. as you know these hyper parameters are the only things which are successful data centres will be guessing when creating a particular model. these play a huge role in the model such as even a slight difference in learning creates of the box might result in the model training time. So as it will take a longer time to Train having a large amount of data using the particular data set that these all things are what data scientist or machine learning engineer keeps in mind while creating them all let's create our own new network.

MNIST DATASET

Here we are going to use the MN is DDS a. So the MN IC data set consists of 60,000 training samples and 10,000 testing samples of handwritten digit images, not the images are of the size 28 into 28 pixels. the output can lie anywhere between 0 to 9 now the task here is to train a model that can

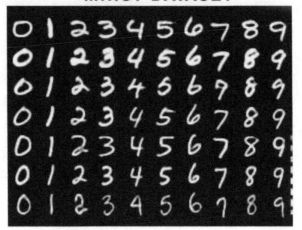

accurately identify the digit present on the image. So let's see how we can do this using tensor fro and Python. So firstly we are going to use the import function here to bring all the print function from Python 3 into python 2.6 or the future statements let's continue with our cone. So next what we are going to do is from pencil for examples tutorials we can take the mi nasty

DEEP NEURAL NETWORKD=

Input image:
28x28 pixels

Input layer:
784 neurons,
one per pixel

Hidden layer:
100 neurons

Output layer:
10 neurons

Output:
predicted
digit value

7

data which is already provided by sensor flow in their example tutorials data but this is only for the learning part and later on you can use this particular data for more purposes for your learning now next what we are going to do is create MN ist . we're going to use the input data tour tree data set and one hot is given us through here. So we're going to import sensor flow and whack plot lib next what we are going to do is define the hyperparameters here. So as I mentioned earlier we have few hyperparameters like learning rate equals batch size display step is not a very big hyperparameter to consider here but. So the learning rate we have given here is 0.001 training epochs is 15 that is up to you because more than the number of epochs the more time it will take for the model to Train. here you have to make a decision between the amount of time it takes for the model to train and give the output versus the speed again we have the batch size of 100 now this is one of the most important have a parameter to be considered because you cannot take all of the images at once. create the radius. So you need to do it in a bath size manner and for that, we define a bad size of 100. So out of 60,000, we're going to take 100 as a bath size 100 images which will go through 15 iterations and the training set has 60,000 images. So you do the math how many batches we will require and how many epochs for each batch we'll have 15 a box the next step is defining the hidden layers. the input and the classes. So for input layers have taken 256 numbers these are the number of perceptron I need or the number of features to be extracted in the first layer.

So this number is arbitrary you can use it according to your requirements and your needs. So for simplicity, I am using two bits X here and the same I'm going to use for the hidden layer 2 now for the number of inputs I'm going to use 784. that is why because as I discussed earlier the MST data has an image or the shape 28 cross 28 which is 784. So, in short, we have 784 pixels to be considered in a particular image . each pixel will provide an immense amount of data. So I am taking a 784 input and number of output classes Here I am defining ten because the output can either range from zero one two three four five six seven eight and nine. So the total number of classes or the output classes here I'm going to use are ten and again we are going to create x and y variables X for the input. Y for the output classes now as you can see here we have the multi-layer perceptron in which we have defined all the hidden layers and the output layers. So the layer one will do the addition and first I will do the matrix multiplication of the weights. the input with the biases and then it will provide a summation and then again the outward for this one will be given to layer two by using the activation function of rail you here. So as you can see here we have rail you activation function for layer 1 layer 2 will take the input of layer 1 with the weights provided in h2 hidden to layer with the biases of the b2 layer it will do the multiplication of layer 1 into weights it will add the biases. then again we'll have a rail lu activation function and the output of this layer 2 will be given to the output layer. So as you can see here in the final output layer we have matrix multiplication of layer 2 into weights of the output layer plus the biases of the output layer and what we're going to do is return the output. So let's mention the weights and the biases. So here we are taking random points for that . next what we're going to do is use the prediction of the multi-layer perceptron using the input weights and biases. one thing more important what we're going to do here is defining the cost. So we're going to use the TF naught reduce mean and we are using the short max cross-entropy with logits this is a function and here we are using the atom optimizer rather than the gradient descent optimizer with learning rate provided initially. what we're going to do is minimize the cost. So again we're going to initialize all the global variables and we have two arrays for cos history and accuracy history. to store all the values and train our model. So we're going to create a session. the training cycle for epoch in the range of 15 we first initialize the average cost at zero. the total patch is the MN asset in the number of examples divided by bass has which is 100 and we loop it over all the patches run the optimization or the backpropagation and the cost operation to get the lost value and then we have to display the logs per each Ipoh for that will show the epochs. the cost at each step we're going to calculate the accuracy add the last to the correct prediction and will append the accuracy to the list after every epoch we will append the cost after every epoch because that is what. we have created cos history and the accuracy history for that purpose and finally, we will plot the cost history using the matplotlib. we'll plot the accuracy history alSo and what we're going to do is we're going to see how accurate is our model. So let's train it now and as you can see at first epoch we have cost 188 and the address is 0.85. So if you see just have the second epoch the cost has reduced from 188 to 42 now it's 26 as you can see the accuracy is increasing from 0.85 to 0.909 one you have reached five epochs you see the cost is diminishing at a huge rate which is very good. you can use different types of optimizers or gradient descent or be it atom optimizer and not go to the details of the optimization because that is another half an hour or one hour to explain to you guys what exactly it is and how exactly it works. So as you can see till the tenth epoch or 11th epoch we have cost 2.4. the accuracy is 0.94. let's wait for a little further till the 50th epoch is turn. So as you can see in the 15th eat walk we have cost 0.83. the actress is 0.94 we start with cost 188 and accuracy 0.85 have you ever east the accuracies of 0.94. So as you can see this is the graph of the cost it started from 188 ending at 0.8 3 we have the crop of the accuracy which started from 0 point 8 4 or 8 5 2 all the way to zero-point nine four. So as you can see the 14th epoch reached an accuracy of 0.9 4/7 as you can see here in the graph again . in the 15th epoch we came to the accuracy of 0.9 for now one might ask the question the accuracy was higher in that particular epoch why has the accuracy decreased another important aspect or have a parameter to consider here is the cost the lower the cost the more accurate will be your mod. So the goal is to minimize the cost which will, in turn, increase the accuracy. finally, accuracy here we have a 0.9 for tonight which is very good now this was all about deep learning neural networks. sensor flow how would create a perceptron or deep neural network what are the different hyperparameters involved how does a neuron work. So let's have a look at

131

the companies hiring these professionals these data professionals in the data science environment we have companies all the way from startups to big giants. So the major companies here we can see as our Dropbox Adobe IBM we have Walmart who were chasing LinkedIn Red Hat there are. So many companies and as I mentioned earlier the required for these professions are

COMPANIES

high but the people applying are too low because you need a certain level of experience to understand how things are working you need to understand machine learning to understand deep learning you need to understand all the statistics. property and that is not an easy task. So you require at least 3 to 6 months of rigorous training with minimum one to two years of practical implementation and project work I would say to go into a data science career if you think that's the career you want to go.

DATA SCIENCE MASTER PROGRAM

So Yurika, as you know, provides data science master program we have a machine learning master program but as you can see in the data master program we have Python statistics we have our statistics we have data size

DEEP NEURAL NETWORK

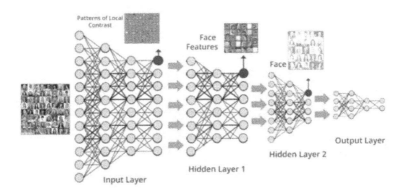

using our Python for data science we have Apache Spark. Scylla we have PA and deep learning with sensor flow we have tableau. So, guys, as you can see here we have 12 courses in this master program with 250 hours of interactive learning via capstone projects . as you can see here we have a certain

DATA SCIENCE MASTER PROGRAM

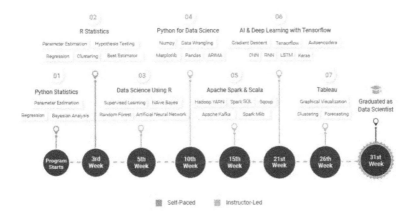

discount going on the hike in salary you get is much more if you go for data science rather than any other program. So you can see we have Python statistics a statistics data science using Python we have Python for data science Apache Spark. Scala which is a very important part in data science you need to know what the Hadoop ecosystem we have deep learning with sensor flow you have tableau. this is a 31 feet course as I mentioned earlier it's not an easy task. you do not become a D assigned all in one month or in two months you cry a lot of training. a lot of practice to become a data scientist or machine learning engineer or even a data analyst because you see a lot of topics on a vast list of areas is what you need to cover. once you cover all of these topics what you need to do is select an either which you wanna work the kind of data which you're going to be handling whether it be text data it would be medical records if it's video audio or images for processing it is not an easy task to become a data scientist. So you need a very good. a very correct path of learning to become a real scientist. So, guys, that's it for this session I hope you enjoyed the session and got to know about data science the different aspects of data science how it works all the ways to either from statistics probability machine learning deep learning. finally coming to AI so this was the path of data science and I hope you enjoyed this session. if you have any queries regarding the session or any other session please feel free to mention it in the comment section below. we'll happily answer all of your queries till then thank you and happy learning.

THE END

www.ingramcontent.com/pod-product-compliance
Lightning Source LLC
Chambersburg PA
CBHW031222050326
40689CB00009B/1443